Lent in Plain Sight

A Devotion through Ten Objects

JILL J. DUFFIELD

WESTMINSTER
JOHN KNOX PRESS
LOUISVILLE · KENTUCKY

First edition
Published by Westminster John Knox Press
Louisville, Kentucky

20 21 22 23 24 25 26 27 28 29—10 9 8 7 6 5 4 3 2 1

Book design by Sharon Adams
Cover design by Eric Walljasper
Cover photo by Louise Lyshoj on Unsplash

Library of Congress Cataloging-in-Publication Data
Names: Duffield, Jill J., author.
Title: Lent in plain sight : a devotion through ten objects / Jill J. Duffield.
Description: First edition. | Louisville, Kentucky : Westminster John Knox Press, 2020. | Summary: "God is often at work through the ordinary: ordinary people, ordinary objects, ordinary grace. Through the ordinary, God communicates epiphanies, salvation, revelation, and reconciliation. It is through the mundane that we hear God's quiet voice. In this devotion for the season of Lent, Jill J. Duffield draws readers' attention to ten ordinary objects that Jesus would have encountered on his way to Jerusalem: dust, bread, the cross, coins, shoes, oil, coats, towels, thorns, and stones. In each object, readers will find meaning in the biblical account of Jesus' final days. Each week, readers encounter a new object to consider through Scripture, prayer, and reflection. From Ash Wednesday to Easter, Lent in Plain Sight reminds Christians to open ourselves to the kingdom of God"-- Provided by publisher.
Identifiers: LCCN 2019050485 (print) | LCCN 2019050486 (ebook) | ISBN 9780664265465 (paperback) | ISBN 9781611649802 (ebook)
Subjects: LCSH: Lent--Prayers and devotions.
Classification: LCC BV85 .D84 2020 (print) | LCC BV85 (ebook) | DDC 242/.34--dc23
LC record available at https://lccn.loc.gov/2019050485
LC ebook record available at https://lccn.loc.gov/2019050486

Contents

Introduction 1

Week One: Dust 3

 Ash Wednesday 5

Week Two: Bread 17

Week Three: Cross 41

Week Four: Coins 65

Week Five: Shoes 89

Week Six: Oil 113

Holy Week: Coats, Towels, and Thorns 137

 Maundy Thursday: Towels 151

 Good Friday: Thorns 154

 Holy Saturday: Thorns 157

Easter Sunday: Stones 160

Introduction

God works through the ordinary. Ordinary people, everyday objects, things we bump up against moment by moment. From burning bushes to talking donkeys to a booming voice from heaven, God goes to great lengths to communicate with people, sending Jesus Christ, God's only Son, to unmistakably tell human beings about salvation, grace, and reconciliation. People of faith report epiphanies, revelations of God's word to them, sometimes by way of miraculous interventions or otherwise inexplicable happenings, but often and also through the mundane made holy due to timing and perception. The note from a friend arrived with the right words, just when encouragement seemed utterly absent. A deer appeared as if out of nowhere, after a voiced prayer for a sign.

Often it is in hindsight that God's providence becomes recognizable and events previously considered mundane become evidence of God's presence and work in our lives. The question for us becomes: Do we have the eyes to see

God's near presence? Do we have ears to hear the word of the Lord, spoken in a multitude of ways and languages? Will we open ourselves to the holy not only in heaven but also on earth and right in front of us? Can everyday objects remind us to stay awake and pay attention?

This Lenten devotional invites readers to open themselves to the kingdom of God, which is close at hand and in our midst. These forty days beckon people of faith to a nearer following of Jesus and an awakening to the work of the Spirit in their lives and in the world. Each week of this book highlights an object, something we encounter in our daily living—things like coins, shoes, and crosses—and asks readers to consider through these objects the possibility, the promise, that God is present, speaking, seeking to be in relationship with them.

I hope this book opens our eyes and ears to the certain providence and power of God, allowing us to lower our anxiety about the future, lessen our burdens about the past, and free us to follow Jesus in faith right here and now. Perhaps if we truly trust that Emmanuel, God with us, never abandons us, we will worry less and risk more for the sake of the gospel. Perhaps when we see a stone or hold coins in our hands or pour out oil into a pan, we will remember that God loves and leads, transforms and heals, guides and intervenes in ways that offer us abundant life, an abundant life we are called to share with others. Perhaps contemplating these ten objects will enable us to see God everywhere, in all things, all creation, not just during these forty days of Lent but every single day of the year, honing our sense of the holy to the point we feel God's presence every single moment and act accordingly.

Jill Duffield
Summer, 2019

Week One

Dust

Ash Wednesday

Genesis 2:4b–7 Psalm 119:25–32

Then the LORD *God formed man from the dust of the ground, and breathed into his nostrils the breath of life; and the man became a living being.*

Genesis 2:7

Dust That Clings*

I have held the last of what remains of an earthly life in my hands, whole people now only ashes, years of living reduced to fine rubble, relationships, work, dreams packaged in a plastic bag to be scattered, buried, or put in a concrete square or ornate urn. Time after time, the wind has blown or I have brushed my hand against my side leaving a trace of the remains on my black robe of ritual sackcloth. It used to bother me, as I did not want those gathered to think I had carelessly handled the dust to

*Reprinted with permission from the *Presbyterian Outlook*. This essay first appeared as "Remembering: An Ash Wednesday Reflection" on the *Presbyterian Outlook* website, pres-outlook.org, on March 1, 2017.

which their loved one had returned. Eventually, I came to welcome the inadvertent imposition, a mark of the communion of the saints clinging to me as I worshiped.

Every Ash Wednesday I think of them, those who've gone to the grave, no longer needing to remember the reality of human finitude we speak plainly each year on the first day of Lent. I think about those I looked at in the eyes and said, "Remember that you are dust and to dust you will return," and then commended at their gritty restoration, "ashes to ashes, dust to dust." I miss them. I remember them even as I remember the One who gives us the sure and certain hope of the resurrection.

I remember not only that I am dust and to dust I shall return, but I cling to the memory of those who've gone before me even as they have clung to the hem of my impotent garment. I remember because that cloud of witnesses gives me hope that I, too, might run the race set before me and that someone, someday, will wear symbolic sackcloth while wrapped in a band of resurrection white and pray I be recognized as a sheep of the fold of the Good Shepherd, a good and faithful servant who has finished her race.

As the dust and ash is imposed on me, forcing me to see my myriad of limits, I remember. I remember I am surrounded by the household of God, sinners redeemed by grace, limited like me, but ever seeking to imitate Christ, however poorly. I remember that I am incapable of doing the good I know but am forgiven anyway. I remember that even as I have shaken the dust from my feet in haste and without just cause, the Holy Spirit has sometimes blown the dirt on my head that I had thrown at others. I remember that repentance means turning away from myself and toward Jesus. I remember that nothing angers God more than rituals of penitence unaccompanied by actions of love. I remember that this Lenten journey is not only about giving up something, but also about standing up for someone. I remember that my years on earth will come to an end and that, God willing, my works will follow me and, thanks to the journey Jesus is embarking on, I don't need those works to save me.

Even as sin clings as closely as the gray remnants of ash on our foreheads, mercy surrounds us like a dust storm stirred up by the relentless wind of the Spirit. Remember. Repent. Turn and follow Jesus Christ, singing alleluia even to the grave until God raises Him from the dead and we are overcome with resurrection joy.

Questions for Reflection

1. As you begin this Lenten journey, whom do you remember? Who has walked with you when you have reached your limits and helped you get through that difficult season?
2. Why do we need to be reminded of our finitude, our dustiness? How does God work within and through our limits?
3. When you encounter dust this week, as you walk, in the wind, or on the side of the road, remember that you are dust, given life and breath by God, and give thanks for the day, the hour, the moment.

Ash Wednesday Prayer

Lord God, giver of our every breath, as we begin our Lenten journey, send your Holy Spirit to blow the dust off whatever in or around us needs new life. Remind us of our limits so that we will once again experience your limitless power. May the ashes on our foreheads prompt us to live our lives in the shape of the cross so that even when the ashes have been washed away, others will see in us the face of Christ. Amen.

Thursday

Job 30:16–23

"And now my soul is poured out within me;
days of affliction have taken hold of me."
Job 30:16

Ground to Dust

The pain of Job's cries resounds through history in the laments of faithful people in every generation. Like Jesus from the cross, sometimes we encounter situations that cannot help but elicit from us the question, "Why, oh God, have you forsaken me?" One of the strangely packaged gifts of Lent is the invitation to lay our souls bare before God. Like Job, like Jesus, like the psalmist and the prophets, we, too, demand God to account for the circumstances that confound our understanding of a good and faithful God.

When we hear of news across the globe of innocents suffering, or we learn of a terminal diagnosis of a loved one, or we struggle with our own inability to get out of bed in the morning, we shout with Job, "I have become like dust and ashes. I cry to you and you do not answer me; I stand, and you merely look at me" (vv. 19b–20). Do something, God! Intervene. Give a sign. Speak in a way that is undeniable and clear.

God's silence echoes in the stillness of our grief and we feel ground to dust. St. John of the Cross describes this state in *Dark Night of the Soul*: "a dense and heavy cloud overshadows the soul, distresses it and holds it as if it were far away from God."* In the presence of this absence time seems unmoving and the darkness seems impenetrable. Life becomes an unending Lent with no alleluias uttered.

Escaping grief, loss, and suffering is impossible. When faced with inexplicable circumstances, asking "Why?" and "How long, O Lord?" and "Where are you, God?" are faithful prayers. When nothing remains of hopes or health, dreams or relationships, but dust and ashes, Lent offers the space to grieve unabashedly and without apology or embarrassment. And yet Sunday, the day of resurrection, cannot be stopped from coming. Alleluias may remain stuck in our throats, but nonetheless rebirth is proclaimed. Resurrection is promised even when we find ourselves weeping by the tomb.

If you find yourself in a dark night of the soul, know you are not alone there. Job is with you. St. John of the Cross as well. Thérèse of Lisieux and Mother Teresa, too. No other than Jesus abides with you there, in the wilderness, in the Garden of Gethsemane, and on the cross. Know, too, that like Lent, this season does not last forever. From the dust and ashes will come new, good life, because the forty days of Lent do not include Sundays, and Sundays, like the light of Christ, cannot be thwarted, no matter how deep the darkness.

*Saint John of the Cross, trans. David Lewis, *The Collected Works of St. John of the Cross*, vol. 2 (New York: Cosimo Classics, 2007), 115.

Questions for Reflection

1. Have you ever experienced a "dark night of the soul"? Were there glimpses of light in the midst of it? How did it impact your faith? Your understanding of the character of God?
2. Take a few minutes to pray for those who may be feeling ground to dust this day. If you are feeling ground to dust and can muster no words of prayer, read aloud Psalm 23 or another passage of Scripture that is meaningful to you.

Prayer for the Day

Gracious God, when we cry to you and feel as if you do not hear us, grant us a tangible reminder of your promise to never leave us alone. When we feel ground to dust, unable to sing your praises or whisper a prayer, surround us with others who will sit with us, pray for us, and be the hands and feet and face of Christ to us. When the night has past and we see the coming dawn, help us to bear the light of Christ to those who still sit in deep darkness until we all shout alleluia on Easter morning. Amen.

Friday

1 Samuel 2:1–10

"There is no Holy One like the LORD,
no one besides you;
there is no Rock like our God."
1 Samuel 2:2

Raised Up from the Dust

Hannah sings of the great reversal that comes as a gift from God, promised and yet unexpected. Hannah prayed fervently, pouring out her heart, so much so that Eli the priest thought her drunk. Confronted for her inappropriate behavior in worship, Hannah holds nothing back from the priest, telling him she had been "speaking out of my great anxiety and vexation all this time" (1 Sam. 1:16). Eli, moved by her pain, tells her to go in peace, adding his hope that the Lord will grant her prayer for a child.

God does indeed grant her petition; Samuel is born and then Hannah prays this song to the Lord. Hannah prayed in her grief and she prays in her joy. Her prayer of anxiety and vexation focused on her own suffering, but this prayer of praise includes all who suffer. The feeble, the poor, the needy, all of them God will raise up from the dust and make sit with princes in seats of honor. No one will be left in the ash heap. Hannah's mourning turned to dancing encourages anyone still desperate or destitute to keep hope—God will not forget you or leave you brokenhearted.

When we are in the ash heap, looking up and around is almost impossible. All we can do is get through the day the best we can. Doing so uses all our emotional resources, with nothing left over. But when we start to feel our burdens lifted, when God raises us from the dust, we begin to notice the pain of the world. Our season of suffering grants us a hard-won empathy that expands not only our prayers but our actions as well. We know we are unable to fully rejoice in our great reversal until everyone has experienced relief from sorrow, too.

Reaching back to help raise others from the dust becomes the unexpected ministry of unwanted days in the ash heap. Countless times I have witnessed Hannah's song enacted in community. The cancer survivor walking alongside the newly diagnosed. The person now sober for twenty years sponsoring a neighbor, who is anxiously attending AA for the first time. One woman I know works tirelessly on suicide prevention because she knows the unspeakable pain of burying her child who took his own life. Even when we've been raised from the dust there are ashes that still cling closely, and we cannot forget those still mired in them.

Hannah's song gets sung again and again when those who have been raised from the dust don't forget what it is like to be consumed with anxiety, perplexed, and covered in ashes. Hannah's prayer of praise gets mixed with the prayers of the suffering, bolstered by Eli's word of peace and lifted from the dust when, in our gratitude for relief, we come alongside others until they are upright, too.

Questions for Reflection

1. Read each verse of 1 Samuel 2:1–10 aloud and notice which verse or verses stand out to you. Use that verse as a breath prayer throughout the day. Make note of any observations or insights that breath prayer calls forth.
2. Must this "great reversal" entail both the bringing up of some and taking down of others? Why or why not?

Prayer for the Day

God of great reversals, you bring transformation, relief, peace, and joy in ways and at times that are utterly unexpected. When we find ourselves in the ash heap, grant us your peace, assure us of your promises, give us a glimpse of hope to sustain us. After we have been raised up from the dust, never let us forget what it was like to be so down. Use our remembering to reach back and help others, to sit beside them until they too know the grace of your transforming love. Amen.

Saturday

Luke 9:1–6

"Whatever house you enter, stay there, and leave from there. Wherever they do not welcome you, as you are leaving that town shake the dust off your feet as a testimony against them."

Luke 9:4–5

Shake Off the Dust

Why are Jesus' instructions to his followers so clear and simple and yet so complicated and difficult? I cannot remember the last time I packed light, let alone took nothing, when setting out on a journey. Nor do I say to myself as I start my day, "Well, good, I have all power and authority over demons and can cure diseases, best get to healing and proclaiming God's kingdom." My days begin and end with much less lofty goals. Getting everyone out the door to their respective places and myself up and ready counts as a win. Not hurting anyone in my orbit often remains an elusive goal.

But Jesus says take nothing, you have the power of God. What more could you need? Also, don't worry about where to lay your head, nor whether you are well received. Go where you are welcomed, move on where you are not. Shake the dust from your feet and keep going. Would that we could let go of rejection, failure, grudges, and anxieties by simply shaking the dust from our feet and trying again.

If I can't leave all I own behind, though, could I let go of just a little? Give up some of the extra baggage I have carried and moved around for years? Lent affords us a time of giving up and letting go, not just of things, but of emotions that weigh us down, too. Guilt rarely moves us closer to the kingdom, neither does shame or vengeance or grudges. Maybe, just for a day, I could leave that bag of ill feelings toward someone at home and see what it is like to walk around the world without having to carry it, drag it, keep track of it.

If I don't imagine I can cast out demons or stand up to villains like a superhero, would it be possible to apologize and ask forgiveness from someone I have injured, thereby, if not stamping out evil, at least creating space for good to grow?

Could I, at least for today, shake the dust off my feet, look forward, keep moving, and simply try again to bring healing where I am able, share and show the Good News wherever I am, and let God take care of the rest?

Questions for Reflection

1. What staff, bag, bread, or extra tunic do you need to leave behind so that you can travel unencumbered today?
2. Is there dust you need to shake off? Something you need to turn over to God in order to focus on the journey ahead?

Prayer for the Day

Lord Jesus, you give us simple, clear instructions and yet we complicate matters and fail to follow them. Forgive us for ignoring your teachings and going our own way. Help us this day to leave behind those things that prevent us from following you. Grant us the power to bring healing and proclaim the kingdom in ways that invite all we encounter to shake off the dust of pain they carry, confident that you welcome us and give us what we need. Amen.

Week Two

Bread

First Sunday of Lent

Matthew 6:7–15

"Give us this day our daily bread."
Matthew 6:11

Daily Bread

"Oh, it's warm!" As I said the words I've said countless times, "The Body of Christ, broken for you," the woman in front of me tore a small piece of bread from the loaf and exclaimed under her breath, delighted, "Oh, it's warm!" The round loaf in my hands was indeed warm, freshly baked and placed on the table just minutes before the Sunday morning worship service started. The smell of bread wafted through the small, country sanctuary. The Communion table laden with silver trays exuded formality, but the bread, warm and less than perfectly shaped, told the story of human hands, earthly grain, and the daily love required to feed people.

I once calculated how many lunches I will have packed for my three children by the time they graduate from high school. Three children, thirteen years of school each, approximately 180 days a year, equals 21,060 sandwiches made, apples washed, chips bagged, napkins packed (some with notes written on them). Never did I imagine so much of my life would be spent packing lunches, planning meals, shopping at the grocery store, cooking. Making sure those we love have their daily bread takes time, effort, energy, thought.

Some days I liked the result and they did, too. Many days the daily bread I served was met with no less grumbling than that of the Israelites in the desert. Rarely did one of my children thank me for the effort or offering. Never did I tuck those juice boxes into their lunch boxes needing their appreciation. I *wanted* to feed them, grateful to have the means and ability to do so. But one day recently I came downstairs to discover my youngest, now a junior in high school, making her lunch and her sister's, too. They were discussing the ideal ratio of peanut butter to jelly, noting their personal preferences: one likes more jelly, the other more peanut butter. One turned to me and said, "Mom, you know the perfect amount of each." The other agreed. "Yes, you make the perfect peanut butter and jelly sandwich."

Who knew? Practice does indeed make perfect, I guess. In that moment I felt delighted. Surprised by the appreciation of such a simple, daily act, one completed over and over again out of necessity, yes, but also love. We need our daily bread. We need to eat, but we are sustained not just by the bread, but by the love with which it is made and given. We come to the table expecting to be fed but are sometimes surprised by how we are nourished with the care that went into the preparation of the bread and the appreciation with which it is received. We exclaim with joy, "Oh, it's warm!"

Questions for Reflection

1. Who prepares or provides your daily bread? Be mindful of each meal today and give thanks for those who nourished you with food, care, and love.
2. When have you been responsible for feeding others? What was that like for you? What are some meals that are memorable to you? What made them so?

Prayer for the Day

Lord, give us this day our daily bread and keep us mindful of those who need to be fed. As we eat and drink, serve or are served, help us to be thankful for giving and receiving. We remember with gratitude all of those who nourish us with food, care, and support. May the daily bread we receive enable us to nurture others in your name. Amen.

Monday

Exodus 16:4–12

"I am going to rain bread from heaven for you, and each day the people shall go out and gather enough for that day."

Exodus 16:4

Bread from Heaven

"Bread from heaven," my friend would say when something needed appeared, be it money to pay a bill or a dress on sale in her size. "Bread from heaven!" "God is good and right on time!" I, in my privilege, would ascribe such happenings to luck, or wouldn't ascribe them to anything at all. Yes, the dress on sale is in my size and darn if it doesn't look good on me, too. Today is my lucky day, I would think or say, or simply take it to the counter and pay, gratitude not part of the process.

My friend who talked about being "too blessed to be stressed," and told me when I expressed worry to "give it to the Lord in prayer" saw bread raining down from heaven everywhere. School supplies donated to the PTA:

bread from heaven. A parking spot close to the building on a rainy day: bread from heaven. A job offer, rebate, or help with her kids, all bread from heaven. While I admired her ability to see downpours of loaves, I confess I also inwardly rolled my eyes and wondered if she was stretching the biblical metaphor. After all, if you read the account in Exodus, the morning manna came predictably every day, from God, not unexpectedly out of nowhere.

Moses told the people God would provide all the bread they wanted, and God did. They didn't get an inadvertent overpayment from the electric company in the mail on the very day the rent was due, in just the amount they needed. They got exactly what they expected, day after day. They even came to complain about the repetitiveness of the provision before long. They took it for granted and wanted more and other. They forgot to give thanks, be surprised by grace, delighted by tangible signs of care, profuse in their gratitude. They got complacent and comfortable and forgot that everyday bread from heaven is worth rejoicing over every single day. They forgot that bread from heaven should surprise us every single day. They came to forget that everything, absolutely everything, from dresses to job offers, from breath to a day at the beach, is, in fact, bread from heaven, a gift, a blessing, something worth celebrating.

A truth my friend knew well. I think I'll call her and thank her for her bearing witness to God's grace and goodness, for being a model of gratitude and joy, for reminding me to put away my grumbling complacency and give thanks instead. I have not talked to her in a long time. She'll probably tell me I called at just the right moment. She'll tell me God is good and right on time. She may even say of my call: Bread from heaven.

Questions for Reflection

1. When have you thought of something as "bread from heaven"? What was it? Why did you label it as such?
2. What do you take for granted? Today try to see everything as a gift from God and give thanks. Make note of how you feel as you do so. How was the day different as a result?

Prayer for the Day

God of heaven and earth, in you we live and move and have our being. Everything we have comes from you, every breath, every moment, every relationship, every provision. The earth is yours and all that is within it. Help us this day to marvel at your lavish care for us and hear our thanks as we gather the bread from heaven you give us every single day. Amen.

Tuesday

Mark 7:24–30

"Sir, even the dogs under the table eat the children's crumbs."

Mark 7:28

Breadcrumbs

Just crumbs, God. Crumbs of your grace and power are enough to heal and sustain. I don't need a whole loaf or a basket filled, only the tiniest of morsels can satisfy the deepest longings of my heart. I'm not asking for myself. I am begging on behalf of those unable to ask you themselves: the children, the sick, the imprisoned, the incapacitated. If you allow me to scoop up the table scraps that have fallen to the floor, I will carry them to those who most need to know they are not forgotten. Is that too much to ask, Jesus?

The story of the Syrophoenician woman, that double outsider, brings up in me a hurt that feels almost primal, a wound of being dismissed, unseen, unvalued. She comes to Jesus on behalf of her daughter, marginalized times four: girl, child, foreigner, sick. If this little girl is not the "least of these" Jesus says are his, who is? But Jesus dismisses this desperate mother, turns her away with a quip about dogs not eating the children's food, the children who are worthy, not her baby. Does Jesus truly not care about the Syrophoenician woman or her daughter? Has even the Son of Man grown callous to those outside his tribe? No matter how many times I read this story, I am angered and puzzled by Jesus' response to suffering. I am chastened by his response as well, because I too often turn away from hurt, desperation, and pain, eager to pretend the need is not my concern.

But this mother, she persists. She refuses to give in to the powerful narrative that tells her she and her family don't matter. She will not go away, nor respond in kind. Her dignity in the face of humiliation astounds me. She accepts the label, derogatory and degrading, but says, even so, I deserve your regard, your care, your power to heal. Just crumbs. Is that too much to ask, Jesus? For me, for my child?

Now is it Jesus' turn to be taken aback in this story. She did not slink away in fear or come back at him with anger. She stood her ground, told her truth, and asked for what she needed. She asked and she received, but it took mountain-sized faith to not back down. Jesus, it seems, sees her courage and then sees her. More than a Syrophoenician: a woman, a mother, a person worthy of his regard, care, and concern. Someone willing to accept crumbs, but for whom Jesus came to be the bread of life. Even that is not too much to ask, not of Jesus.

Questions for Reflection

1. Are there people we disregard and think are unworthy of our concern? Who are the outsiders, the exponentially marginalized, in our context?

2. Have you ever begged God for help for yourself or on behalf of another? What happened?
3. As you see crumbs or table scraps today, consider who is in need of our care and consider how you might offer them more than leftovers.

Prayer for the Day

Lord Christ, as we go about our daily work and routines, help us to truly see those in our midst who are too often dismissed or disregarded. Forgive us for the times we have acted as if the suffering of our fellow human beings was not our concern. Grant us the faith to offer abundant grace, mercy, and compassion, much more than crumbs, in your name. Amen.

Wednesday

Ecclesiastes 11:1–6

Send out your bread upon the waters,
for after many days you will get it back.
Ecclesiastes 11:1

Bread on the Water

Cast your bread upon the waters, sow seed in the morn-ing, and go about your life and work recognizing that much of what comes our way is a mystery, unpredictable, often more than we imagine, sometimes painful in ways we could never predict. These verses in Ecclesiastes call forth questions of fate, chance, luck, and providence. Popular culture has co-opted the concept of karma from Eastern religions, pointing to instances when we believe someone gets what's coming to them. The preacher of Ecclesiastes will not let us go that route, however. (Satis-fying as such just desserts may be to us.)

Casting your bread upon the waters, sowing seed in the morning, and working with diligence engenders humility, not a cynical attitude resigned to fate or itching for karma or looking for a lucky break, but hopeful assurance that God provides and sustains, often in ways we could not foresee. Has this not been true in your own experience?

God promises to uphold us. Jesus says he will not leave us orphaned. We are given an Advocate, the Holy Spirit, to comfort and guide us. Jesus himself prays for us. Paul reminds those early Christians that when we plant and water gospel seeds, God will indeed give the growth. Casting our bread on the water, and sowing seed, while not always offering an instant return, is always a sure investment in the divine economy of grace and mercy. But doing so requires trusting the God who gives breath to our bones enough to let go. We must be willing to throw our bread on the water even when we do not have any idea how it will come back to us. We must scatter those gifts with which we are entrusted, knowing that God will use them in ways beyond our hopes and imagination, but perhaps beyond our time and ability to see the results.

A life of casting bread on the water is a life of patience and long views, and such characteristics do not get lauded in a culture of quarterly returns and instant messaging. Daily, diligently, we are called to ask ourselves: Of what do I need to let go in faithfulness and for the sake of the gospel? What bread should I cast on the water today? These questions invite us to lean into God's promises of provision, God's certain providence, and the confession of faith that Jesus is Lord of all. Our lives are not left to luck, fate, karma, or chance; we believe in the Triune God who creates, redeems, and sustains. Therefore, we cast our bread on the waters with abandon and with joy, trusting the One who rules heaven and earth, to use it and bring it back to us, a beautiful mystery, divinely certain, humanly impossible to fully understand.

Questions for Reflection

1. What do you need to let go of today? What bread do you need to cast on the water?
2. When have you had bread that you have thrown on the water returned to you?

Prayer for the Day

Lord of sea and sky, heaven and earth, your promises are sure and your providence certain. Help us to trust you enough to cast our bread upon the waters with joy and scatter gospel seed with abandon. Take what we offer you, bless and use it to provide for those longing to be fed, physically and spiritually. Thank you for the countless ways you provide for us every day. May we be grateful and generous in response. In Christ's name we pray. Amen.

Thursday

John 6:1–14

"There is a boy here who has five barley loaves and two fish. But what are they among so many people?"
John 6:9

Barley Bread

A large crowd versus a boy with five barley loaves and two fish. A large, hungry crowd versus twelve disciples. A large, hungry crowd, twelve nervous disciples, one boy, five cheap loaves of bread, two fish of unknown size, and Jesus. The math we do, the calculations we figure in our heads, may well be mathematically, logically correct, but the figures do not add up when compared to the power and compassion of the Messiah. Why is it so hard for us to trust in God's ability to provide even in the face of inexplicable odds?

We continue to scratch our heads and plead with Jesus to send people away because we don't have the capacity to feed, house, hear, serve, love this huge crowd. Just look around! We cannot possibly be expected to satisfy the deep longings of so many. Six months' wages wouldn't begin to put a dent in the poverty, suffering, complex challenges of this mass of humanity on the hillside, right?

Well, right. But Jesus can do more than we hope or imagine with the small resources we willingly give to him in faith. That's the lesson we need to be taught over and over. Jesus does not ask of us that which we do not have. He instead receives what we offer, takes, blesses, uses, and multiplies our five loaves of less-than-gourmet bread, the two fish we caught after hours of fishing, our ability to pray, our adeptness with numbers, our knack for sewing, our passion for words, our joy in writing notes to people. All we need do is to be like the boy, to bravely step forward in the middle of intimidating circumstances and offer to Jesus whatever we have on any given day. Jesus takes it from there.

Have you experienced a "loaves-and-fishes" miracle? I once traveled to a small, rural town ravaged by floods and met with a group of faithful people who felt compelled to help their neighbors in the wake of devastation. The food pantry they'd recently started became the hub of relief efforts in their county. Within days of the receding waters, the large building they previously wondered how they would use overflowed with every manner of supplies, from canned goods to cleaning products. Their enthusiasm overflowed through the building, too, as they recounted how repeatedly they prayed for a need to be met and, as if miraculously, it was.

"We had jars and jars of peanut butter, but no jelly, so we prayed for jelly. On the very next truck there came jars and jars of grape jelly."

"We needed water and darned if within hours people came with donations of water."

Repeatedly, offerings came that eased the suffering of hurting crowds. People bringing whatever gifts they possessed, offering them willingly, disciples distributing them until all were fed, with baskets left over.

Questions for Reflection

1. Do you find it hard to believe that God can and will provide? Why or why not?
2. When have you experienced a "loaves-and-fishes" miracle? What happened?
3. What are your five barley loaves and two fish? What gifts are you called to offer to Jesus right now?

Prayer for the Day

Lord, forgive us for how easily we forget that you have the power to do more than we can ever hope or imagine with whatever gifts we freely give to you. Help us to boldly step forward in times of need and offer ourselves for your service. Take, bless, and use our barley bread, our fish, our desire to serve in ways that bring relief to those who are suffering. May we too look upon the crowd with compassion. Amen.

Friday

John 6:35–40

"I am the bread of life. Whoever comes to me will never be hungry, and whoever believes in me will never be thirsty."
John 6:35

Bread of Life

"I am the bread of life." These words of Jesus seem alternately mundane and cryptic. The other "I am" sayings resonate with mystic poetry. "I am the way, the truth and the life." "I am the light of the world." "I am the resurrection and the life." "I am the good shepherd." Perhaps "I am the door" does not exactly soar, but at least we understand the metaphor. Jesus the bread of life, of course, resonates with sacramental language. We cannot help but think about the Lord's Supper when he utters these words. Unlike the twelve disciples, we know what will come in the days ahead. We understand the inextricable link between the bread of life and the soon-to-be crucified and resurrected body of Jesus. Even so, do we consider Jesus to be the staple of our very existence? Our sustenance without which we would surely perish?

When full days and crammed calendars represent routine seasons punctuated with times of greater or lesser stress, often thinking about my need, daily, for Jesus slips my mind. I readily recognize the importance of electricity, food, clothing, bill-paying, and transportation. I often forget the words of that hymn "Just Give Me Jesus." I neglect the truth of God's great faithfulness that reveals new mercies morning by morning. I strive for those things that moths destroy, and expend the bulk of my energy acquiring them, or worrying that I don't have enough of them stored up, or worrying about maintaining, securing, protecting what is stored up. I forget that Jesus is the bread of life.

Jesus assures us: "I am the bread of life." Therefore, we need not get ourselves in a tailspin of acquisition, a relentless spiral of coveting, a meaningless pursuit of so much that advertises fulfillment but leaves us always hungry for more. Just give me Jesus. Just give me the bread, the body of Christ, that offers life, abundant and eternal. Fill me till I want no more and nothing else.

Jesus' words, his identity, "the bread of life," reveal the promise and truth that in the ordinary, necessary staples of life, he is present. Jesus assures us that regardless of our striving after that which thieves steal or our gorging on what amounts to empty calories or our obliviousness to the holy provisions all around, the bread of life sustains us, nourishes us, never runs out, and blesses us even when we neglect to return thanks.

Questions for Reflection

1. When have you felt hungry, physically, or spiritually? What satisfied your hunger?

2. Do you think about Jesus daily feeding and sustaining you?
3. What is life-giving for you? How do you experience Jesus in those life-giving moments?

Prayer for the Day

Jesus, bread of life, you sustain us through seasons when we fail to feel your presence. You nourish us when we fear we cannot keep going. You feed us when we are hungry for purpose, hope, and healing. You assure us that when we believe in you, we will never hunger or thirst again. You promise us that you will never abandon us. Therefore, we ask: Just give us yourself and we will be satisfied. Amen.

Saturday

1 Corinthians 11:17–26

"This is my body that is for you. Do this in remembrance of me."

Bread That Is Christ's Body

Paul holds nothing back, giving that band of Christians in Corinth a piece of his mind as only he can. "What?! You think I am going to praise you? I don't think so!" Paul received word that when the Corinthians gathered around the Lord's Table, divisions were evident, factions present, acrimony on the menu. Further, some would hog the food or show up drunk, and not everyone ate and drank equitably. Nothing praiseworthy here. Christian table manners require a vastly different kind of behavior.

Remember that we eat the bread, the body of Christ, in remembrance of the One who died for us, poured himself out for us, kneeled and washed our feet, and instructed us to do likewise. We eat from the one loaf and drink from the one cup, reminding us that we are one in and through Christ Jesus our Lord. When we gather at the Table of the Lord, our relationship with Christ dictates our relationships with each other. United in Christ we look back and remember the life, death, and resurrection of our Lord, and we anticipate his coming again. That anticipation calls for readiness to meet him face-to-face at any moment. Not drunk and divided, fractured and fatigued, but unified in love, outdoing one another in service, rejoicing that in Christ there is no longer Jew nor Greek, slave nor free, male nor female, but Christ is all and in all.

When we eat the bread that is Christ's body, we experience a foretaste of the heavenly banquet to come, when all tribes and nations gather together, worshiping and singing alleluia together. How often, when we celebrate Communion, do we remember that the whole communion of the saints celebrates with us? How often do we honor Christ's saving death until he comes again by reconciling with those who come to the Table with us, those still far off, and those we made feel unwelcome?

Paul speaks not only to those early Christians in Corinth. He admonishes us, too. He sees the divisions, factions, and selfish behavior present in our fellowship, and he says, "In this I will not praise you." He calls on us to examine ourselves, confess our sin, repent, and repair our relationships so that we do not eat in an unworthy manner, taking for granted the sacrifice of Jesus Christ, who died in order that we might be made one with him and through him with God and one another.

Questions for Reflection

1. How do we examine ourselves before we come and eat the bread that is Christ's body at the Communion table?

2. How do we balance our need to confess with the truth the Christ welcomes us even though we will never be worthy?
3. Are there relationships you need to try and repair? Divisions and factions that need to be healed? Hold these in prayer this week and then do what you can to make amends.

Prayer for the Day

Gracious God, you welcome us to the Table of our Lord even when we can never be worthy to sit at the table with the One who knew no sin and yet took on ours. When we take for granted the amazing grace offered in the bread of Christ's body, cause us to stop, examine ourselves, and instead approach with humility and awe. May our life together reflect the reconciliation won for us through Christ's sacrifice. Amen.

Week Three

Cross

Second Sunday of Lent

Mark 8:31–38

"If any want to become my followers, let them deny
themselves and take up their cross and follow me."
Mark 8:34

Take Up Your Cross

The sequence for discipleship begins with denial of self,
moves to taking up one's cross, and then journeys to following Jesus. The steps seem important; one cannot happen without the prior action being done. Letting go of
selfish ambitions, ego, and self-protection precedes taking up the cross which Jesus requires. Following Jesus
minus the cross does not constitute discipleship, instead
merely spiritual curiosity or a free, no risk, cheap grace
trial of apostleship, or perhaps aloof reporting on the
oddity of this Jesus of Nazareth. Denial of self, taking up
the cross, and following equal the trinity of discipleship,
the three-legged stool of faithfulness, the doing justice,
loving kindness, and humble walking of singular loyalty
to the Most High God.

But how do we define our cross? What exactly does Jesus mean when he instructs us to take up our cross? If doing so is not simply the burden of human finitude: illness, a challenging family member, a tragedy or hardship, what does Jesus call us to carry? Perhaps, if we are struggling with aspects of Jesus' command, we need to return to the first step and deny ourselves, look outward, look to Jesus. The cross taken up by Jesus leads to taking on the sin of the world, a sacrifice for the sake of others, a willing relinquishing of status, power, safety, and security. Might ours entail such qualities, too?

We are not Jesus, of course. Some of us hold great status, power, and security. Some of us hold little or none. And yet, all of us wield influence in whatever circles we inhabit. In those circles, big or small, with that influence, obvious or under the radar, do we actively choose to look past our self-preservation and risk our own interests for the sake of the vulnerable, oppressed, marginalized, and fearful? When we do, we weave together the trinity of faithful discipleship, denying ourselves, taking up our cross, and following Jesus.

Denying ourselves, taking up our crosses, and following Jesus may not be as dramatic as martyrdom, but it could be. It may be as simple and difficult as standing up to those with whom we are closest when solidarity with them would keep us safe. It could be advocating for those without a voice even when doing so alienates us from those in power. No matter the end result, daily standing on this three-legged stool of a solid Christian life prepares us to follow Jesus all the way to Jerusalem, and bears witness to him along the route to all we encounter along the way. Working for justice and being just, loving kindness and being kind, and walking humbly as we follow Jesus make for a life of purpose and joy, strangely synonymous with self-denial and cross-bearing.

Questions for Reflection

1. What are your spheres of influence? How are you using your influence in those spheres?
2. Do you own items of clothing, jewelry, or art with a cross? Why? What do those items mean or symbolize to you?
3. When have you denied yourself as an expression of your faith in Jesus Christ?

Prayer for the Day

Lord Jesus, you denied yourself, took up the cross, and journeyed all the way to crucifixion in Jerusalem. We confess that we resist self-denial, we refuse to take up the cross that requires sacrificial love, we fail to follow when your way challenges our comfort and safety. During this season of repentance and reflection, help us to more closely, more willingly, more nearly imitate you. Amen.

Monday

Hebrews 12:1–3

Consider him who endured such hostility against himself from sinners, so that you may not grow weary or lose heart.
Hebrews 12:3

Look to the Cross

Looking to the joy before him, Jesus endured the cross. Jesus, the one who pioneers and perfects our faith, disregarded the shame and torture of the cross and now sits in glory at the right hand of God. Jesus' example, the book of Hebrews argues, should inspire and guide us in our own faith, life, thoughts, actions, hopes, and longings. Jesus' model of sacrificial love combined with that of the great cloud of witnesses spurs us forward despite our fatigue and doubts. We look to the cross, that instrument of death, humiliation, and stark warning, for inspiration and assurance. Sometimes the oddness of Christianity cannot be denied. The cross, designed by the state to instill terror and illicit subjugation, for us calls forth words of radical forgiveness and inexplicable grace and the freedom found only in Christ.

Looking to the cross reminds us of Jesus' promise of the peace that passes understanding, but also convicts us of the cost paid for the gift of the peace of reconciliation with God and neighbor. Too easily we move from glory to glory, from Jesus' healings and teachings to his resurrection appearances and ascended glory. We look to the cross for inspiration to endure the costs of discipleship, to remember that Jesus bids us come and die. Redemption came through Jesus' suffering and crucifixion, rendering the cross an instrument of resurrection life, and putting an end to death. That's why we keep running the race set before us, no matter how uphill the path sometimes feels.

While I was riding in the car with my daughter, out of nowhere she asked, "Do you know what really bothers me?" "No," I said. "It really bothers me when people don't know the difference between a cross and a crucifix." I did not expect this to be on the top of her adolescent list of irritants. Her frustration stemmed from a pop culture reference that, to her, revealed a lack of basic religious knowledge. But as I thought about it, I began to consider the theological importance of that very distinction. We Protestants look to the cross, not the crucifix. The cross devoid of the body of Jesus spurs us forward to the joy set before us—resurrection, yes, but also the undeniable assurance that death does not have the final word. Jesus does not remain fixed forever in death on the cross. The powers and principalities of this world do not, will not, have the last word. Jesus Christ has taken his seat at the right hand of the throne of God, worshiped by a great cloud of witnesses, all of them praying for us, cheering us on, urging us to keep running the race of faith and living a life that reflects the character and will of the pioneer and perfecter of our faith until we join them in glory.

Questions for Reflection

1. What or who spurs you on in faith when you are lagging or uncertain? Do you think about the cloud of witnesses that surround you? Write down some of their names and give thanks for them.
2. How do the cross and joy go together? What shame do we need to disregard in order to be faithful?

Prayer for the Day

Lord Jesus, pioneer and perfecter of our faith, we thank you for refusing to give up on us and on the world. You gave up your very life for our sake, pouring yourself out completely so that even the cross could be transformed into a means of life and grace. We seek now to run our race of faith encouraged by the promise of seeing God face-to-face and joining in worship with the great cloud of witnesses. Amen.

Tuesday

1 Corinthians 1:18–25

For the message about the cross is foolishness to those who are perishing, but to us who are being saved it is the power of God.

1 Corinthians 1:18

Foolishness of the Cross

Expectations of God's coming Messiah were many and varied. Most of those expectations included military might and an overthrow of those who had oppressed God's people for far too long. None of those expectations included a cross, a public and humiliating death, weakness and defeat. Human beings revere winners: the strong, the powerful, the famous, even the dishonest, clever criminal who somehow escapes the consequences of her actions. Those oppressed, downtrodden, and at the mercy of those in power do not envision and hope for a savior to meet the same fate as they did. No wonder Paul says both Jews and Greeks see the cross as foolishness, a stumbling block, a scandal. Jesus, a poor carpenter from some backwater village, pulls together a small group of uneducated fisher-men and despised tax collectors, garners a following of desperate crowds, gets himself in trouble with secular and religious leaders, and ends up executed for all to see. Who would see God at work in such a failure? Who would see God as such a loser?

Only the formerly perishing who have been saved through this Jesus' life, death, and resurrection recognize God's glory in Jesus' defeat. Only those like Paul who have been struck blind, rendered helpless, surrendered, and been given new eyes to see. Only those twelve who have seen their teacher and friend, once dead, now alive, wounded, scarred, but breathing the Holy Spirit. Only members of the crowd who have lunged at the hem of his garment and been healed, called out for mercy and been heard, handed over a pitiful piece of bread and seen it miraculously feed thousands. In short, only the foolish.

God rarely meets our expectations. The cross is proof enough of that. God inevitably exceeds all we could ever hope or imagine, rendering our plans utter foolishness. God in Christ reveals a wisdom we can never attain on our own and a power made perfect in weakness. We har-bor hopes for revenge, Christ desires mercy. We want success, Jesus tells us to be servants. We stay up thinking about how to get even, Jesus commands we love our ene-mies. We hold grudges, Jesus says forgive seventy times seven. All of this godly wisdom seems so foolish: there is nothing more powerful than vulnerable, sacrificial love. No wonder we prefer a sign or some worldly wisdom. But once we've been redeemed by such foolishness, all we ever want to be is a fool for the One who saved us.

Thankfully, God uses what is weak in this world to show forth divine strength. God takes the broken and unwise, the formerly proud persecutors of the gospel, the uneducated, the ignorant, the despised, the needy, all manner of human beings who really thought they wanted signs and status, and uses them to bear witness to the saving power of the cross—God's foolishness that silences any earthly wisdom.

Questions for Reflection

1. Have you ever experienced your wisdom being rendered foolishness in the face of God's plans and purpose?
2. When have you demanded a sign from God? Did you receive it? Was it what you expected?
3. How are you a fool for Christ?

Prayer for the Day

God of wisdom and power, we get caught up in the wisdom of this age, wanting you to fulfill our desires even when they do not reflect your will or wisdom. Forgive us for demanding anything other than the foolishness of the cross. Help us to rest in the saving power of Christ's cross so that we can be a fool for him until he comes again in glory. Amen.

Wednesday

Philippians 2:1–11

And being found in human form,
he humbled himself
and became obedient to the point of death—
even death on a cross.

Philippians 2:7b–8

Death on a Cross

"If there is any encouragement, any consolation, any sharing, any compassion and sympathy, make my joy complete and live in a way that demonstrates the unity won for us in Christ Jesus our Lord" (Phil. 2:1–2 au. paraphr.). This passionate plea in Philippians feels urgent, as applicable today as it no doubt was to the Christians in Philippi. Be who you are. Show love. Regard others as better than yourself. Exercise humility, deference, look to the interest of others. In short: Be like Jesus.

Perhaps not so much WWJD: What Would Jesus Do, but BWJI: Be Who Jesus Is. An impossibly high standard, yes, and yet the only standard to which we should aspire.

Utterly countercultural. Absolutely perplexing to those outside the circle of faith. A cruciform life makes for an odd shape in an ethos awash in consumerism, competition, and tribalism. Look to the interest of others. Practice humility. Let the same mind be in you that was in Christ Jesus. What mind was that?

The mind that, though he was in the form of God, emptied himself totally, obedient to the point of death on a cross. Memorize Jesus' life and emulate it. Put in the forefront of your mind the mind of Christ who gave up everything for us. Be mindful of the people around you, unfurl yourself, look up and out and around and ask: What do compassion and sympathy look like right here, in this situation, right now? What would it look like to give myself away on behalf of another? In light of the truth that Jesus, the Son of God, came down from heaven and went all the way to death on a cross, how should we live together? How can we work for accord in a culture fraught with ever-increasing division and animosity?

At the very least, look to the interests of others, a small but significant imitation of Jesus' death on a cross, who looked to the interest of all of creation. Practice in small things, keeping in mind that those who are faithful in little are faithful in much. Not to trivialize Jesus' death, but for those of us who will inevitably fall short of the glory of God, making small efforts that Jesus can bless and use strengthens the synapses of our Christ-like mind. Let that person ahead of you in traffic. Be the first to apologize. Tip generously. Make the call, send the note, ask that beleaguered person if they are all right. None of these come close to the death on a cross of our Savior but each honors his sacrifice and attunes our minds and hearts to the world he so loves. All contribute to the joy of the body of Christ.

Questions for Reflection

1. What does it mean to have the mind of Christ?
2. Does being of one mind mean agreeing with one another? If not, what does having one mind mean?
3. How can you look to the interests of others today?

Prayer for the Day

Lord, we will never, ever have the same mind of Christ. His sacrifice, love, and compassion can only inspire us to respond with humility, looking to the interests of others in ways that often feel trivial. Yet we trust that you will take whatever we offer in faith, bless, break and use it in ways that nurture others, bring joy, and show your love. Amen.

Thursday

Colossians 1:15–20

He himself is before all things, and in him all things hold together.

Colossians 1:17

Reconciled through the Cross

Tensions increased with each phone conversation. A face-to-face meeting was impossible due to geographical and emotional distance. The miles of separation were symbolic of the gulf in the relationship. A decision made by one family member precipitated a division of opinions on the part of the other members of the family. Taking sides became inevitable. Reconciliation was out of the question. Finally, the communication came: she does not want to talk to you, at least not for a while. The proclamation brought searing pain along with odd relief, not unlike a bandage being quickly pulled off a wound. Maybe some air would bring healing, even if a scar emerged.

Estrangement, hurt, arguments, division: every family, every congregation, every group encounters the challenges of life together. When we invest deeply, we inevitably struggle mightily to maintain our connections to one another. The temptation to stop talking, walk away, resort to our own corners, takes over sometimes. Separation seems like the best option, the only way to preserve ourselves or some semblance of survival. Reconciliation? Impossible. At least for a while.

During those days of agonizing unraveling, be it divorce or a bitter argument, an inability to forgive, or the guilt of knowing our actions damaged a person we love, the cross of Jesus Christ holds the hope of healing as yet unrealized. Jesus Christ himself bore all things; in him all things hold together. Despite the painful reality that all things on earth, in our lives, in our families and churches, at times fall apart, the cross of Jesus holds all of us and all our chaotic circumstances together. Through the cross of Christ, God was pleased to reconcile to God's self all things. *All* things. The scars on Jesus' hands, his feet, his sides show us that no wound is too grievous for God to heal and make whole, reconciliation never impossible now that peace has been made through Jesus' blood on the cross.

Not all human estrangement ends in a joyous reunion, like Joseph weeping on his brother's neck or Esau running to meet Jacob with forgiveness, not vengeance. Divorce happens. Congregations spilt. People refuse to speak to each other and take grudges to the grave. But we know not even the finality of death thwarts the love of God. The cross of Christ holds all things together, brings all things together, draws us all, in the end, together. When the ache of broken relationships or disappointment in ourselves or others reigns, we cling to the hope of the reconciliation of the cross, knowing that Christ has borne all sin, and therefore reconciliation, no matter how remote, how hard, how improbable, is undeniably possible on earth and in the fullness of time, and ultimately inevitable in heaven.

Questions for Reflection

1. When have you experienced division and estrangement? If reconciliation occurred, how did it come about?
2. Are there relationships that you are called to work on for reconciliation? What would facilitate healing?

Prayer for the Day

Lord Jesus, you hold all things together. Hold us together this day. The places of hurt, the hurts we have perpetrated, the wounds that seem to fester rather than heal, in all our pain, whatever its form, bring wholeness, peace, relief. If we cannot as yet reach across the chasms we have created, then, for now, draw us close to you so that our proximity to you brings us closer to each other until we experience fully the reconciliation won for us on the cross. Amen.

Friday

Mark 15:16–24

They compelled a passer-by, who was coming in from the country, to carry his cross; it was Simon of Cyrene, the father of Alexander and Rufus.

Mark 15:21

Carrying Jesus' Cross

"They compelled a passer-by." The word *compelled* sanitizes what happened to Simon of Cyrene. Imagine the scene for a moment: Simon, walking down the street, perhaps headed to work or home or to the market, hears a commotion. He looks around and sees Roman soldiers forcing a man, bruised and battered, down the road. The man, bent over under the weight of a cross, wears a crown of thorns. Simon, coming from the country, knows the fate of the pitiable man—painful execution. Simon, no doubt, has passed by convicted criminals on crosses before and knows enough to stay out of the way of the Roman guard, unless compelled—forced—to do otherwise.

Could Simon have refused? Why did the soldiers compel a bystander to carry Jesus' cross? I always wonder if Simon's act was one of compassion or complicity. Is it possible that shouldering Jesus' cross part of the way could be both? Three of the four Gospel accounts of Jesus' passion record Simon of Cyrene bearing Jesus' cross. The recording of the details of Simon's name and location point to the importance of this act, compelled or not. The disciples fled. Jesus' closest followers did not follow him to the cross, despite his repeated command that anyone who wished to come after him must deny themselves, take up their cross and follow. Does that anyone now include Simon? Simon, willingly or not, gets swept up in God's salvation story, forever inextricably connected to the passion of Christ. Even Roman soldiers and passersby further God's plan when disciples refuse to participate.

God's will to save the world cannot be denied. Disciples of Jesus can deny they know him, repeatedly. The twelve then and the countless now may refuse to deny themselves and take up their crosses, choose to save their own lives rather than lose them for Christ's sake. Regardless, Jesus goes to the cross, forgives them anyway, and saves the world. Even those compelled into service, oblivious to the role they are playing or the one they are serving, further the will of the God who never gives up on the beloved creation.

Simon of Cyrene, compelled passer-by, embodies the power of God to use any of us, all of us, despite our ignorance, fear, and reluctance. Some days our faith compels us to follow Jesus wherever he leads. Many days we run away and deny we ever knew Jesus. God's salvation story unfolds every day. Our acts of compassion cannot be unwound from our complicity with sin and sinful systems.

God uses them anyway. Our complicity with oppressors and oppression is not devoid of God's grace and mercy. Simon reminds us that the cross of Christ will be borne and the world redeemed by the One we try to follow, too often deny, and always seek to worship.

Questions for Reflection

1. Imagine yourself as Simon of Cyrene. What are you thinking and feeling? How does the experience of carrying Jesus' cross change you?
2. In thinking about your own faith story, have there been times you willingly took up the cross? Times when you were compelled to do so?
3. Could Simon have refused to carry Jesus' cross? What difference does it make if he did or didn't have a choice?

Prayer for the Day

God of power and might, you work through us and often despite us. We turn from the suffering of Jesus and the suffering of others. We fear for our lives and act in self-protective ways, neglecting those vulnerable and in danger. Forgive our unwillingness to lose our lives for Christ's sake. Make us willing servants of your will, and when we turn and run, by your grace, use us for your work anyway. Amen.

Saturday

Mark 15:25–32

Those who passed by derided him, shaking their heads and saying, "Aha! You who would destroy the temple and build it in three days, save yourself, and come down from the cross!"

Mark 15:29–30

Come Down from the Cross

Utter defeat. Humiliation, suffering, helplessness. The scene is painted of Jesus on the cross, hung between two bandits, the sign above him and crown on him marking his "kingship." Those walking by taunt him. Even the criminals being crucified with him deride him. Nothing about this image shows hope or power or divine providence. I find solace in the disciples' inability to see their Master brought so low, shamed and tortured. I am relieved they ran away. Reading these verses makes me want to turn the page and skip to the resurrection. Disciples then did not know this was not the ending. In the face of such cruelty, is it any wonder they abandoned Jesus?

I long for Jesus to come down from the cross, give those who hurt him their due, show the passers-by and the promulgators of violence alike that God does not tolerate hate, dehumanizing, and murder. I want this scene to play out like one in a comic book, a superhero movie, recompense and victory coming just as the hero looks doomed. Come down from the cross, Jesus! Reveal without ambiguity the goodness and power of the Most High God. Show them who is boss!

But Jesus remains on the cross, dying and derided. What kind of God do we worship?

We worship the God who refuses to leave any person, place, or circumstance forsaken and irredeemable. We worship the God whose power is made perfect in weakness. We worship the God who forgives the very ones who taunt and torture, deride and degrade. We worship the God whose vulnerable, sacrificial love takes on the sin of the passers-by and soldiers, criminals and Caiaphas, Pilate and persecutors, followers who turn back, disciples who deny, and women who refuse to leave.

We worship the God who remains on the cross regardless of the cost, in order to save the world.

I desperately want Jesus to come down from the cross. I want the Holy Spirit to swoop in and the voice of God to boom from heaven. I want a comic book, superhero ending, but I worship a God committed to remaining on the cross until God's plan for salvation is finished, complete. I worship the God who remains on the cross and remains with us no matter how painful the circumstances. I worship Jesus Christ, the One who refused to come down from the cross so that all will be lifted up by it and nothing can separate us from the love of God.

Questions for Reflection

1. Read this text and picture the scene. What enables people to be cruel to those already suffering?
2. History records the lynching of African Americans by white Christians on church grounds. How do religious people then and now justify their violent behavior? How do we prevent this perversion of faith?
3. Do you ever want God to orchestrate a superhero-type ending to events? How do we remain faithful in the midst of painful circumstances that do not have an obvious victorious ending?

Prayer for the Day

God of the cross, you endure cruelty, withstand taunts, refuse to come down and seek revenge. We long for double recompense, you offer inexplicable forgiveness. We want public karma, you extend demonstrative grace. We wish you would show your power with unambiguous payback, instead your strength is made perfect in sacrificial love. As recipients of your mercy, saved through your vulnerability, shape us more and more in your image. Amen.

Week Four

Coins

Third Sunday of Lent

Mark 12:13–17

But knowing their hypocrisy, [Jesus] said to them, "Why are you putting me to the test? Bring me a denarius and let me see it."

Mark 12:15b

Image on the Coin

If Jesus is Lord of all and the earth is the Lord's and all that is in it, how can anything truly belong to the Emperor? Jesus, once again being tested by those who seek to harm him, answers a trick question with an honest answer. This group of Herodians (a sect of Hellenistic Jews) come to Jesus with disingenuous affirmation and ask: Is it lawful to pay taxes or not? Jesus, on to their tactic, poses a question back to them: Whose head and title is on the coin? They answer what is obvious: the emperor's. Well then, Jesus says, give those coins—pay your taxes—to the emperor and give God God's due.

What about the first commandment to love God with all our heart, soul, mind, and strength? What about losing our lives? What about leaving everything to follow Jesus? Does anything truly belong to the emperor? Questions of paying taxes pale in comparison to the requirements of discipleship. Questions about turning over the coins in our pockets mask the real struggle of giving our entire lives to God.

Look at the coins in your wallet or pocket. Who is on them? George Washington, Thomas Jefferson, Abraham Lincoln. What do these men represent? What do we owe them? Should they be worshiped? Admired, or lamented, or both? What about the national symbols on the other side of those coins? The eagle, Monticello, the Lincoln Memorial. Are these symbols and places worthy of ultimate loyalty? How about the words and phrases? "Liberty." "In God we trust." Values to which we aspire, or rhetoric we have failed to fulfill, or both?

The reign of emperors ended. We live in a democracy where elected officials do not demand worship and yet commitment to politics and loyalty to political party borders, if not trumps, our religious beliefs. Too often we have made politics, the images on the coin, ultimate. The question that followers of Jesus must ask is not, "Should we pay taxes?" but rather, "Are all our loyalties and everything we value penultimate to the Lord of all?" The Herodians come to Jesus to test him. Followers come to Jesus not with faux flattery but with sincere questions, not to trick but to learn. Jesus teaches both Herodians and disciples: Pay taxes to whoever is on the coin, but never imagine that those people and symbols imprinted thereon should be worshiped, unquestionably revered, or ever placed before the One to whom we give our life, our all.

Questions for Reflection

1. Notice the coins that pass through your hands today. Look at the words and images and consider how they reflect the gospel and how they contradict it.
2. Where do you place your ultimate loyalty? What things, ideas, or even people are you tempted to put before God?

Prayer for the Day

Lord of all, we come to you with questions that reflect our own priorities and wrongly ordered priorities. We act as if coins and country trump your will and ways. Forgive us for falling into idolatry. We seek instead to come to Jesus with sincere praise, honest questions, and teachable spirits so that our loyalty will be to you alone. Amen.

Monday

Luke 15:8–10

"What woman having ten silver coins, if she loses one of them, does not light a lamp, sweep the house, and search carefully until she finds it?"

Luke 15:8

Lost and Found Coins

She rejoices in random pennies found on the ground. Dimes, nickels, and quarters cause delight, too. The monetary value of the coins does not elicit the praise, just the discovery of a shiny or dirty, newly minted or long in circulation coin. The finding alone brings great joy. Shared joy. Not that she shouts out, "Eureka!" when she spots the copper amidst the gravel of the grocery store parking lot. She stoops to pick it up, says a silent prayer of thanks, and slips it in her pocket or decides to leave it for another in need of a blessing on that particular day.

I know this only because she's shared with me her practice. The found coins, unknowingly lost by others, remind her of God's presence and providence. She sees the dime peeking out from beneath the kitchen counter as a God nod, a talisman not of luck but of grace, enough currency of mercy to keep her moving ahead in faith on days when hurts of the past threaten to paralyze her. Her vision of lost coins found and the ensuing gratitude has transformed my own sight. I no longer disregard the penny rattling around the dryer or the nickel at the bottom of my purse. Each one brings to mind a mini-alleluia, an inaudible "thank you," and a moment of recognition that I am not alone.

Even in places already sacred, coming upon a coin grants a holy pause. On a recent Sunday I settled in our family's usual back pew. Distracted by many things, I bowed my head to catch my breath and attempted to focus. Upon opening my eyes, I saw gleaming on the hundred-plus-year-old wooden floor planks a penny. Funny, I thought, I did not see it previously. Surely the coin had been there all along, but in my haste, I'd not seen. But there it shone, right in front of me. How could I have missed it?

The prelude began but I continued in a posture of prayer, picked up the penny, the present year stamped on it, and wondered how it had landed on the back pew of this old country church. This small congregation met only on the Sabbath; likely no one had darkened the doors or sat in this pew since we'd occupied it the week previous. The pews were affixed to the floor with solid slats the entire length of the bench, so there's no way the coin could have rolled from a parishioner further up. Maybe it had strayed from the offering plate or been kicked unknowingly down the aisle. Regardless of how the penny landed between my feet, I rejoiced in knowing that no matter where it had been or how long it had been lost and left, now it was found, not unlike me, in church.

Questions for Reflection

1. Have you ever lost something of value to you? If you found it, how did you feel upon the discovery of it?
2. What small, daily discovery reminds you of God's presence and providence? A penny? A bird? A word or phrase?
3. What has been a cause for such joy that you had to find others to rejoice with you?

Prayer for the Day

God of the lost and found, we rejoice that you seek us out, never give up on us, and throw a divine party when we repent and turn to you. As we go about our day, help us to discover signs of your presence and care. May seemingly small things like random pennies and discovered dimes bring forth praise, joy, and an assurance that you never leave us alone. Amen.

Tuesday

Luke 21:1–4

[Jesus] looked up and saw rich people putting their gifts into the treasury; he also saw a poor widow put in two small copper coins.

Luke 21:1

Two Small Coins

Jesus notices the poor widow. Jesus understands the depth of the sacrifice those two copper coins represent. How many temple goers failed to see her or thought little or not at all of the small contribution she put in the treasury? Jesus saw the woman. Jesus saw her fully. Jesus recognized both her person and her circumstance and held it up to those who no doubt looked past her that day and every day.

While this story is often used in stewardship season as an example of generosity, perhaps a better interpretation requires that we truly and fully see the widow as Jesus did. Putting in all she had, jeopardizing her well-being, may indeed be an example of her piety and faith, but it also reveals a less than flattering aspect of the institution to which she turns over her two small coins. Widows and orphans, the vulnerable and marginalized, should be the very ones the coins in the treasury support, not exploit.

Jesus notices the poor widow and the rich. Jesus understands the impact of both their giving—on themselves, the temple, and the community. Jesus sees the relationship between the poor widow and the rich both going to worship and calls upon those gathered around him to see that relationship, too. The last verse of chapter twenty, which comes just prior to Jesus' pointing out the widow and the rich, denounces the scribes with this indictment: "They devour widows' houses and for the sake of appearance say long prayers. They will receive the greater condemnation" (v. 47).

Jesus is not so much praising the widow's sacrificial giving as condemning those who fail to notice her and see her predicament. God never rejoices in giving until it hurts. Jesus condemns those who devour widows' houses, especially those who do so in the name of the Lord. Television preachers who prey on those desperate and afraid, promising miracles for the right donation, scribes who take the prime seats in the synagogue but neglect to care for the poor, Christians who worship on Sunday and cheat their customers on Monday, Jesus notices them along with the widow and her two small coins. He understands the relationship between the two. He recognizes the hypocrisy of those who feel righteous in their tithing and temple attendance but neglect the poor widow without two coins to rub together. He calls upon those gathered around him, listening, to see the poor widow, truly regard her, and care about her. He calls upon disciples to address the circumstances and systems and institutions that compel her to put all she has to live on in the treasury.

The point of this exchange is not so much about sacrificial giving as it is about communal living, who we notice, whose gifts count, and how the systems all around us impact each and every person.

Questions for Reflection

1. Who are the poor widows in your church and community? Do you notice them?
2. Everyone has gifts to share. How do we invite the people to share their gifts in ways that are life-giving and not exploitive?
3. How do you decide what is faithful to give to the church? Charity? Individuals?

Prayer for the Day

Jesus, we gather around you and ask to hear what you want to teach us today. Who do you want us to notice? What do you want us to do about those right now who have nothing to live on? Help us to give faithfully no matter if we only have two small coins or a large bank account. Help us to see both rich and poor through your eyes and with your compassion. Amen.

Wednesday

John 2:13–22

Making a whip of cords, [Jesus] drove all of them out of the temple, both the sheep and the cattle. He also poured out the coins of the money changers and overturned their tables.

John 2:15

Poured out Coins

The expressions on Jesus' face in the images depicting this biblical account arrest me. I confess I do not like seeing Jesus angry, wielding a whip, chasing people and animals. I prefer the kinder, gentler version of Jesus, the pictures of Jesus with a lamb wrapped around his neck, the 1950's Sunday school curriculum Jesus with children on his lap and seated around his feet. The drawings of Jesus, red-faced and grimacing, vendors cowering in fear, birds' wings flapping, feathers flying, sheep and cattle scattering in terror, they trouble me. Which, I suppose, they should.

Jesus is not always mild and meek. Jesus kneels to wash feet, eats with sinners, soon will submit to the cross. But in this story, he is enraged. So what causes his ire? Were not the people selling cattle, doves, and sheep simply making a living? Providing a needed service? After all, those going to the temple came from great distances to make required sacrifices; they had to buy those animals somewhere. Coins needed to be exchanged so that offerings could be made with the right currency. Why does this seemingly needful activity elicit Jesus' fury?

The answer lies not so much in the "what" as in the "how" of this buying and selling. Buying and selling, providing services—nothing is inherently sinful in such practices. However, when they take advantage of the place, time, and market, Jesus gets mad. When money is loaned at exorbitant rates to those without other options, Jesus forms a whip of cords. When merchants price gouge in the aftermath of a disaster, Jesus starts turning tables. When corporations create fake accounts, add fees, and penalize those unable to pay them, Jesus' anger grows. When worship becomes an occasion for exploiting people, Jesus unleashes his wrath. How we earn and use our coins matters to Jesus. It matters a great deal, in fact. Jesus cares about how we behave not just in the temple but just outside of it and well beyond its doors. Gentile or Jew, merchant, currency changer, or worshiper, how we make our money concerns the Lord of all.

I often wish the ledger of my checking account was off-limits to my Lord. I wish Jesus did not care about whether my purchasing habits impacted the people around the globe who produced the goods I buy. Life would be far less complicated if Jesus allowed me to compartmentalize my economic choices from my spiritual practices. If only I could look at just the images of Jesus with the lamb, the children, and the towel around his waist. But all four Gospels give us the account of Jesus cleansing the temple, and therefore I must reckon with how Jesus regards my relationship to money and whether or not how I make and use it is cause for his anger or praise.

Questions for Reflection

1. Does it trouble you to imagine Jesus angry and wielding a whip? Why or why not?
2. Are there current practices you think elicit Jesus' wrath? Are there current economic practices that should make us angry and that we are called to overturn?
3. Look through your bank statement. How does it reflect your Christian beliefs?

Prayer for the Day

Lord of all, no part of our lives is off-limits to you. You require us to be faithful in little and in much, with our money, our time, and our talents. If there are practices in which we engage that make you angry, send your Spirit so that we will see where we fall short and change our ways. Pour out coins, turn over tables, chase far from us whatever offends you and keeps us from worshiping you in truth. Amen.

Thursday

Matthew 10:26–31

"Are not two sparrows sold for a penny? Yet not one of them will fall to the ground apart from your Father."
Matthew 10:29

Two Sparrows for a Penny

The expanse of God's knowledge and care, God's power and love, cannot be fathomed by those of us made in the divine image. We talk about "compassion fatigue" and burn out, lacking emotional bandwidth, or simply reaching the end of our rope in relationships and otherwise. We project our own human limits on the triune God. Surely, we think, God no longer hears the same prayer we have prayed for weeks if not years. Surely, we imagine, God has bigger problems to tackle than ours—be they health related, family dynamics, money stresses, or job woes. This passage tells us otherwise. God cares deeply for us. So deeply, in fact, that God accounts for every hair on our heads. As the psalmist notes, every word we utter is known to God before we ever even speak it, each of our days numbered, written in God's book.

God's involvement in our lives knows no limits. God's concern for the creation God made and called good did not stop on the seventh day of sabbath rest. No, God refuses to let us alone, comforting and sometimes frightening as such holy purview may be. Jesus so emphatically wants to communicate God's providence and omnipotence and loving-kindness that he points to the sparrows, two sold for a penny, of not much worth from our human perspective. And yet, these sparrows that we buy and sell for next to nothing—God notes the death of each and every one. How much more, therefore, does God regard each and every person?

How might we see ourselves, the people around us and around the globe, animals and all creation, if we considered daily their worth in the eyes of God? When I find myself with a cynical thought bubble above my head or on the cusp of a barely contained eye roll, Jesus' assurance of God's benevolent attention toward me calls me to extend such grace toward others. When I cringe and feel sadness at the sight of the squirrel dead in the middle of my country road, I no longer chide myself for being sensitive but remember that God winced over the suffering of this rodent, too.

I cannot know and care on the scale that God knows and cares. I am a creature. But I, like all creatures, am valuable to God. Knowing that truth, recalling it daily, enables me to see other people, other animals, creation, through a gentler, more loving lens. God counts every hair on my head, and on yours, too. God delights in sparrows and squirrels, butterflies and worms. No portion of land or person, centimeter of earth or centipede, is unseen by our God. All are knit together and known by their Creator.

Questions for Reflection

1. What do we sell for "two pennies" that God cares deeply about? How does this knowledge shape our relationship to those two-penny creatures and things?
2. Are you mindful that God loves you so much that there is nothing about you unknown by God? Take some time today to remember that all your concerns are God's concerns, too.

Prayer for the Day

God, we give thanks for the sparrows sold for two pennies, the squirrels so plentiful we often fail to notice them and for all the priceless people we encounter this day. We thank you, too, for your unfailing love for us. We give to you our deepest concerns and our greatest hopes, knowing that you will take them, honor them, and mold them into something beautiful for you and for us. Amen.

Friday

Ezra 2:64–69

As soon as they came to the house of the LORD in Jerusalem, some of the heads of families made freewill offerings for the house of God, to erect it on its site.

Ezra 2:68

Coins for the Building Fund

After nearly fifty years of exile in Babylon, the Jewish people return to their homeland. The second chapter of Ezra reads like a census and then an accounting ledger. No detail spared, all of these years later we read the names of those making the journey back home—servants and singers, horses, camels, mules and donkeys. Specific numbers given—seven, 337, 736, 6,720—indicate the care the scribe, Ezra, gives to this narrative of God's promise fulfilled. Fifty years of captivity meant some who had marched to Babylon would not be returning to Palestine. Fifty years in a foreign country meant children had been born and grown and had children of their own, none of them knowing the majesty or ritual of the

Temple. Restoration and rebuilding require work, attention to detail, the investment of the entire community, all 42,360 of them.

The first place the assembly goes is the site of the house of the Lord. What remains? Rubble? Remnants of objects once used in worship? Imagine the mix of emotions upon seeing what was once the center of their lives, destroyed, but soon to be restored. In my head I hear the voices of those venturing back to neighborhoods destroyed by fire or flood, looking at all that has been lost but saying through tears, "We will rebuild." The heads of some families make a statement with their resources, put their money where their hope is, and give a freewill offering. Ezra gives us the numbers: "sixty-one thousand darics of gold, five thousand minas of silver, and one hundred priestly robes" (v. 69).

So determined were they to restore the place of worship and the center of their lives, the first thing some heads of families do is put gold and silver coins in the treasury. Like those lead gifts in a capital campaign, these returning exiles model confidence in a yet-to-be-seen future, inspiring others to give according to their resources too. Coins freely given contain the power to cast a vision and shape the future. Generosity begets generosity. Backing our belief in God's promises with our coins, time, energy, and talents demonstrates faith even in the face of rubble, loss, and a whole lot of work yet to do. The donation of priestly robes matters too.

Ezra's detail of the handing over of one hundred priestly robes reminds the whole assembly that worship will indeed happen in the place again. Those robes represent the foresight of one family as they were forced to Babylon. Like refugees and migrants of every generation, they took with them that which they most treasured, and someone said, "Get the priests' robes. We will need them when we come home."

Rebuilding takes coins. Restoration requires robes. The heads of some families inspire the whole assembly. God's promises remain steadfast and those who trust this truth stand on the sight of all that was lost and see possibility, so much so they make freewill offerings with confidence and joy.

Questions for Reflection

1. Have you ever experienced the loss of home or country? If so, what did you take with you or what do you most miss?
2. Read some stories of contemporary refugees. How did they survive their forced exile?
3. When have you made a freewill offering in order to help shape a promised future?

Prayer for the Day

Lord of coins and robes, families and animals, kings and servants, your promises will not be thwarted even when we wonder why you delay in fulfilling them. Fifty years, a hundred, a lifetime, generations, we await with eager longing the day when the lion will lay with the lamb, when crying and mourning will be no more, when your promised restoration will be fully known. Until then, grant us such confidence in you that we keep the priestly robes ready and make freewill offerings daily. Amen.

Saturday

Matthew 26:14–16

*They paid [Judas] thirty pieces of silver. And from that
moment he began to look for an opportunity to betray him.*
Matthew 26:15b–16

Coins of Betrayal

Thirty pieces of silver. That's all it took for Judas to betray
the one who had washed his feet, whom he'd witnessed
heal, feed and tend the neediest of people, and heard
teach about loving enemies and forgiving seventy times
seven times. Thirty pieces of silver in exchange for Jesus.
My grandfather used to say, "People will sell their soul
for a quarter." Or their Messiah for thirty pieces of silver.
Or their integrity for a kickback, bribe, or better position.
Why do we so readily hand over what's priceless for a
meager sum of money—or a major sum, for that matter?

Did money motivate Judas to turn on Jesus? We can
never know. Nonetheless, he took those coins and then
began to look for an opportunity to betray the Son of
God. He sold his soul for a quarter, as my grandfather

would say. A poor rate of return if there ever was one. We read about his treason, knowing the regret that will consume him once the deed comes to pass, and cannot ourselves imagine doing likewise. But how often do we "sell our soul for a quarter" or exchange what is priceless for thirty pieces of silver?

Whatever our family system, our relationship to money cannot help but be complicated. Our consumerist culture relentlessly attempts to persuade us that nothing trumps the value of wealth, the accumulation of coins, the security and status of money. No wonder we give into the temptation to take the silver and turn in our Savior. We're worth it, the billboards tell us. If we don't do it, someone else will. Nice guys finish last. Only the naive play by the rules. It's a dog-eat-dog world. Look out for number one. The one who dies with the most toys wins. Come on, Judas, all you have to do is point him out, what happens next is not your fault or your problem. We'll even pay you thirty pieces of silver. Easiest money you've ever made. What do you say?

While we cannot imagine ourselves as Judas, we should this Lenten season examine how we sell our soul for a quarter, turn over our integrity for a handful of coins, give in to the idolatry of money in ways big and small, come to believe that wealth, not Jesus, will save us. We forget to invest in that which moth cannot destroy or thief steal. We forget that not everything is a commodity that can be bought and sold. We neglect what is truly priceless in our lives, beginning with our own integrity.

The nonnegotiable, exceedingly good news resounding through time for Judas and for you and for me remains the truth that Jesus came to save sinners. He forgives those who betray him. He knows that often we do not know what we do until it is too late, and our regret consumes us. The Messiah's relentless, priceless, not-for-sale mission is redemption. We may sell our soul for a quarter, but Jesus buys it back with his life.

Questions for Reflection

1. While we may not come close to Judas' act of betrayal, in what ways are you tempted to exchange your integrity for much less-valuable commodities?
2. How do we participate in systems with our money that exploit others? What can we do about such practices and systems?
3. What acts have you committed that you deeply regret? Take some time to make amends as you are able and ask God for forgiveness, knowing God is merciful.

Prayer for the Day

We are not Judas, God. We would never betray Jesus for thirty pieces of silver. We would never deny him, either. At least, this is what we tell ourselves. Yet, when we are honest with ourselves and with you, we know we do in fact sell our soul for a quarter, exchange the eternal for the temporal, and fail to invest in the priceless relationship we are granted with you through Christ's sacrifice. Forgive us. Reveal to us that which we do. Help us to recognize what is truly valuable and live accordingly. Amen.

Week Five

Shoes

Fourth Sunday of Lent

Exodus 3:1–6

Then [the Lord] said, "Come no closer! Remove the sandals from your feet, for the place on which you are standing is holy ground."

Exodus 3:5

Take off Your Shoes

Moses stood watch over his father-in-law's sheep. I wonder if, on the day or night the bush caught fire, Moses expected to encounter the Most High God in the middle of a field of sheep? Perhaps, like many of us, Moses relegated the holy to those places designated for worship, set aside for ritual, marked as special and mostly off limits to ordinary people. God, though, refuses to be boxed in by our expectations or designations. God speaks from the clouds and out of the burning bush. God uses everything from angels and donkeys to proclaim, instruct, and admonish us. God alone constitutes the holy. Our role is to respond by taking off our shoes, to recognize the holy when we experience it, to turn aside our gaze in humility, follow instructions, and listen.

I remember the summer I did an internship as a hospital chaplain, young and unsure and not fond of the smell of antiseptic or the sight of blood. Sacred ground rarely came to mind when I walked the halls, visited patients, attempted to make conversation with the nurses. I covered the psychiatric unit. I liked it. The patients stayed longer than those on medical surgical floors and there were fewer visible bodily fluids. At first, knowing that once I got buzzed in, I was locked in along with the patients, felt unnerving but soon it came to seem more like safety than threat. At that time, elderly patients with dementia were admitted to the psych unit until more appropriate placement became available. One dapper gentleman thought I was the waitress at the country club. I regretted I could never bring him his requested Reuben or gin and tonic. I participated in arts and crafts and asked the nurses if I could be helpful. I suspect my ability to be useful was limited, but at least I didn't feel like I was in the way, like I often did on other floors.

Then one day a nurse pulled me aside. A new person had been admitted in the night. The woman was in her late thirties, deeply depressed, and in need, the nurse thought, of talking with a chaplain. I knocked on her door, the room so dark I could barely see the figure curled up on the bed. I told her my name and my role and asked for permission to come inside. I heard a faint "yes." I sat in the lone chair by the bed and after a few minutes the woman began to talk. As she shared her story, she unfurled just a little. Years of depression. Some improvement, then a painful relapse. Different medication. Electroshock therapy. Wanting to give up. Not wanting to hurt her family. As she laid bare her heart, trusting me with her suffering, the well-polished linoleum floors became holy. I knew I could not heal her. I knew enough to listen. To sit patiently and say little. To heed to the Holy Spirit. To pray. To assure her of the presence of God whom I felt was surely in the room with us. I visited her regularly until her doctor discharged her, not cured, but better and hopeful.

In that hospital room I could not take off my shoes, but I could recognize that God made it holy ground. I could acknowledge the unmistakable presence of our God and act with reverence, awe, and thanksgiving.

Questions for Reflection

1. Have you ever experienced holy ground in an unexpected place? What about it made it such? How did you respond?
2. Why did God instruct Moses to take off his shoes? What did his shoes symbolize?
3. Have you ever metaphorically or literally taken off your shoes as a sign of respect or humility?

Prayer for the Day

God of shepherds and sheep, Moses and me, you speak to us through unconsumed burning bushes and unassuming, ordinary encounters. You go to extraordinary lengths to communicate to us, assure us of your presence, enlist us in your service. Give us eyes to see and ears to hear. Show us when to speak up and when to be quiet. Tell us when to take off our shoes and when to put on your whole armor. May all we do today reflect our awareness of your presence. Amen.

Monday

Mark 6:6b–13

He ordered them to take nothing for their journey except a staff; no bread, no bag, no money in their belts; but to wear sandals and not to put on two tunics.

Mark 6:8

Shoes for Mission

Take nothing for your journey. That's what Jesus tells the twelve disciples as they prepare to embark on their first mission trip. Do not take any money; no credit card, cell phone, or snacks. As one who has led mission trips, as one not known for light packing, just reading this passage makes me nervous. The mission trips of my experience involved youth and meetings with parents and lists of what to bring and lists of what *not* to bring, but I never once advised: Take nothing. Jesus does get specific with clothing, however. He doesn't mention rain gear, a warm jacket, work gloves. He doesn't get that specific, but he is detailed nonetheless. Bring one tunic and one pair of sandals. Be unencumbered and ready to move. Do not be weighed down with baggage, literal or figurative, but be open to the hospitality of whoever offers you a meal, a room, a seat at their table, and a place in their home.

Shoes for mission must be sturdy, comfortable, and appropriate for all terrain. Sandals in Jesus' day and climate would have fit that bill. Sandals were easily removed. Dust shaken off. Feet readily washed. Repeat as necessary. Therefore, the wearer could enter and leave a town, a neighborhood, a home without delay, assistance, or fanfare. If we too seek to serve, our shoes should reflect our willingness to go wherever Jesus sends us, to whoever welcomes our word and work. Shoes for mission signal— to the wearer and the ones to whom that wearer is sent— willing participation in the life and work of the place their feet take them. Shoes for mission allow for jumping into a community with both feet.

In his book *You Welcomed Me: Loving Immigrants and Refugees Because God First Loved Us*, Kent Annan tells the story of meeting a man in a refugee camp. This gentleman fled his home with nothing; no bread, bag, or money. He had no choice. He'd had no time to pack. He fled with the clothes on his back and the shoes on his feet. Shoes that now were completely worn out from a long journey and months of farming a small plot of land. Noticing the state of his shoes, Annan offered to trade footwear. The man agreed to try them on and test the viability of Annan's shoes for the daily work and walking he knew would be required of them. He assessed that the newer, intact shoes could fulfill the mission, and the two men swapped.*

*Kent Annan, *You Welcomed Me: Loving Refugees and Immigrants Because God first Loved Us* (Downers Grove, ILL: InterVarsity Press, 2018).

Dressing for mission may call on us not only to pack light, but to give up whatever we have brought on the journey. Shoes for mission must be ready for anything.

Questions for Reflection

1. Have you ever participated in a mission trip? What did you pack and why?
2. How many pairs of shoes do you own? What do you consider when you choose a pair to wear for the day or an occasion?
3. What do you need to leave behind in order to be ready to follow Jesus daily?

Prayer for the Day

Lord Jesus, your clear instructions test our ability to trust you and others. We want to pack items for any conceivable circumstance, store up security in bags, boxes, and storage units. You call us to let go of whatever holds us back from freely going where you send us. You teach us to rely on the hospitality of strangers and the promised provision of God. Today we will leave behind at least some of what encumbers our faithfulness to you and put on shoes for mission. Amen.

Tuesday

Luke 15:11–24

*"The father said to his slaves, 'Quickly, bring out a robe—
the best one—and put it on him; put a ring on his finger
and sandals on his feet.'"*

Luke 15:22

New Shoes

"People get excited about new underwear."

When I asked our youth group what they learned
while serving in various ministries across the city, the
teenager on the mission trip who'd spent the day distributing clothing at a center for those experiencing
homelessness responded, "People get excited about new
underwear." The rest of our band of volunteers giggled,
but I am not sure that was the desired reaction. This
participant tended toward the serious and thoughtful.
Perhaps he did want to impress his peers with a quip
about underwear, but his answer revealed that he had
nonetheless noticed the impact of something everyone
in our group no doubt took for granted. Despite his shy

97

demeanor and reserved manner—he rarely talked in our nightly gatherings—he expanded on his initial impression. "New socks really make a difference too." He paused and added, "And new shoes."

The giggles gave way to a serious conversation. Living on the streets eats away at people's dignity. Walking everywhere not only wears out shoes, it damages feet. Hygiene challenges persist when access to showers, bathrooms, and toiletries is scarce. Used clothing fulfills the purpose of covering and warmth, but who wants used socks or underwear? Doesn't everyone want shoes that are theirs alone? The young man who had distributed clothing that day lamented that there had not been enough new items for everyone, noting the visible disappointment of those who'd missed out. New socks, new underwear, and new shoes could not only make someone's day, they also could enhance someone's health and restore someone's dignity. Sometimes something new signifies that someone is valued, worthy, and noticed.

The familiar story of the Prodigal Son tells of a young man returning home expecting to be shamed or relegated to secondary status, but who instead receives an unmitigated welcome—new clothing, new shoes, and a party. His father sees him, runs out to meet him, and wants only to show him how deeply valued and beloved he is. Grace never does just enough; by definition grace overflows, explodes, exceeds, gratuitously manifests in unexpected ways. Grace is exhibited by embarrassing public displays of affection, weeping in joy, running in welcome, new robes, new rings, new shoes, a huge party where all are invited so that no one could possibly question their value or belovedness. People get excited about new underwear. And new socks. And new shoes. People get excited when their inherent value and dignity, their individuality and their God-given worth, is honored with welcome, celebration, and new shoes, too.

Questions for Reflection

1. When have you experienced a sense of being valued and beloved? How was that expressed?
2. Have you ever been surprised by a gracious response when you expected judgment? Have you ever offered grace to someone expecting your judgment?

Prayer for the Day

God of grace, you run out to meet us in love when we anticipate having to beg for your mercy. You see our uniqueness and know our value as your children. As we bask in your embrace, marvel at our new clothing, and celebrate at the banquet given in our honor, our excitement grows. Knowing the joy of such grace, we look to live in ways that cause your mercy and goodness to explode and overflow into every corner of our homes, community, and world. Amen.

Wednesday

John 1:19–28

John answered them, "I baptize with water. Among you stands one whom you do not know, the one who is coming after me; I am not worthy to untie the thong of his sandal."
John 1:26–27

Not Worthy to Even Tie His Shoes

From his very beginning, John the Baptist pointed to Jesus. We learn in Luke's Gospel that John leapt in Elizabeth's womb at the sound of Mary's voice. Luke tells us, too, that before John's birth he was filled with the Spirit. John's unique role gave him the ability to recognize Jesus as the Messiah well before Jesus began his public ministry. John knew his role as prophet and preparer, the one who pointed always away from himself and toward Jesus. Never did John confuse his call with that of the Savior's. While I would not sign up for John's job (as we learn later in John's Gospel, preparing the way for the Lord can get you killed), I do envy his clarity of purpose.

The priests and Levites ask who he is. They want to know what he says about himself, and without ambiguity or hesitation John tells them—not this, not this, not this, but this. Oh, and by the way, I am not worthy to tie the sandals of the one for whom I am making a way. I suspect not only John's testimony but also his humility got their attention. The virtue of humility stands out in its rarity. As Alan Simpson noted at George H. W. Bush's funeral, "those who traveled the high road of humility in Washington, D.C. are not bothered by heavy traffic."* Never has that highway been a congested one, but clarity of purpose and an unwavering belief in God's call paves the way for a life that inevitably points away from self and toward the divine, a life that prepares a path for the present and coming Messiah.

John the Baptist is singular. But, when it comes down to it, so is each one of us. John came to baptize with the baptism of repentance, to proclaim the coming Messiah, to tell the world, to tell us, to get ready. We are not called to be John the Baptist, and yet we are called by God to prepare to receive Jesus personally and then bear witness to him to the ends of the earth once we do. None of us are worthy to untie the thong of his sandals, either. Pointing away from ourselves and toward God, practicing humility, remembering our status as creatures, beloved and made in God's image, tasked with God-given purpose, a little lower than angels, but never to be confused with the Messiah, makes a way for the holy in our lives and in our world.

*Tim Hains, "Former Sen. Alan Simpson Eulogizes George H. W. Bush," RealClear Politics, December 5, 2018, www.realclearpolitics.com /video/2018/12/05/former_sen_alan_simpson_eulogizes_george_hw_bush .html.

Questions for Reflection

1. What is your God-given purpose? How are you preparing yourself and others to welcome Jesus?
2. If someone were to ask you, "What do you say about yourself?" how would you respond?
3. How is the virtue of humility cultivated? Practiced?

Prayer for the Day

God of glory and majesty, you alone are holy and worthy of our praise. You sent Jesus to save, to show us your ways, to teach us your will, to reveal your love. Forgive us when we fail to point to our Savior, when we forget our role and seek to be more or less than who you create and call us to be. Convict us of your purpose for us and send your Spirit to enable us to fulfill it boldly. Amen.

Thursday

Acts 12:6–11

The angel said to him, "Fasten your belt and put on your sandals."

Acts 12:8

Put on Your Belt and Shoes

God makes a way. The bottom line of this blockbuster story is the fact that God makes a way for the ministry we are called to do on God's behalf and at God's behest. Peter, "bound with two chains, was sleeping between two soldiers, while guards in front of the door were keeping watch over the prison" (v. 6). Nevertheless, he escapes from prison with the miraculous help of an angel. Even Peter thinks such a reprieve unbelievable, only a vision perhaps, until he finds himself, shoes on, belt on, cloak on, solidly outside the prison gates. God makes a way, even when all the facts point to the end, the impossibility of escape, the inevitability of failure. Angels in countless guises appear and tell us to get up, get dressed, put our clothes on, and get ready to be freed.

The challenge for us, or at least one of them, remains trusting God's promise and will to make a way while chained to current circumstances and imprisoned by forces not under our control. Illness, economic hardship, broken relationships, job loss, a fire, flood, or earthquake, addiction . . . the list of calamities that bind us feels endless. Being human means being vulnerable. How, then, do we imagine that God makes a way? Considering Peter's story helps. How much more dire could a future be than the one he faced in that prison cell? But recalling the events of our own lives bolsters our hope in the middle of confusing and confining times even more. Has God not made a way for you when you thought an end, or *the* end, inevitable?

As a wise friend once said, "God keeps God's promises, but always in surprising ways."

Work done to bring a ministry that offers emergency shelter to families experiencing homelessness reminds me of this truth when I am feeling trapped and afraid, doubtful and hopeless. The effort started with three people, then grew to a dozen or so. We recruited the requisite thirteen host congregations. Out of seemingly nowhere came the required day center. Wringing our hands and lifting prayers, a bus donation came through. Just when money was needed, just enough appeared. Over and over, when our faith waned and we could not see a way, God made a way. Now thirty-two congregations host families. When one space for the day center fell through, another space became available. As one of the people who worked on this from the very beginning said, "(T)his building literally falls out of the sky into our laps! It has everything we need and will provide room to grow and perhaps even to expand or consolidate our mission . . . I should have trusted in the Lord! I can't count the number of times . . . with (this ministry) that something like this has happened."*

God makes a way. So put on your belt and shoes, grab your cloak, and let's go.

Questions for Reflection

1. When has God made a way when you thought there was no way?
2. What ministry are you engaged in right now? What are the challenges or impediments? How have you seen God working through them? Has it been surprising?

Prayer for the Day

God, you make a way for the work you call us to do in your name. When we falter and are afraid, bolster our confidence, comfort us in our anxiety, send messengers, angels, and unexpected provisions. Even when we are unsure and doubting, help us to be like Peter, ready to put on our belt and shoes so that we can follow your angel's instruction and be freed to fulfill your purpose for us. Amen.

*Personal email to the author.

Friday

Exodus 12:11–1

This is how you shall eat it: your loins girded, your sandals on your feet, and your staff in your hand; and you shall eat it hurriedly. It is the passover of the LORD.

Exodus 12:11

Shoes for Escape

Tom Kiefer's collection of photographs entitled *El Sueño Americano* (The American Dream) features image after image of items confiscated from migrants crossing the border into the United States.* Once apprehended by Border Patrol agents, "nonessential" items are taken and discarded. Kiefer, who worked for ten years as a janitor at a Border Patrol station, noticed these items, retrieved them, and began taking pictures of them. The images haunt the viewer. Row after row of water bottles; a collection of small, blue New Testaments and Psalms in Spanish; children's drawings; a lone stuffed toy. Extra clothing

---

*Tom Kiefer, *El Sueno Americano*, www.tomkiefer.com.

gets taken by Border Patrol, as do the shoes not on the person's feet. Belts and shoelaces, dubbed potentially dangerous to self or others, get tossed into the garbage, leaving their former owners to go through the court proceedings without them.

The objects reveal the dangerous nature of the journey of escape. Essentials like water to survive the desert heat and shoes that withstand the miles and miles of walking speak to the physical challenges faced by desperate travelers. The rosaries and handwritten notes tell of the spiritual hopes that spur men, women, and children to keep going despite the miniscule odds of making it to the promised land. The toothpaste, nail clippers, and combs remind us of the universal basic human need for hygiene and dignity. The row after row of baby food jars defies words and simply moves me to prayer.

People fleeing horrific circumstances take little with them. They must take needed items for survival, thinking carefully about shoes that protect, make for easy movement, and are sturdy enough to withstand difficult terrain for a long period of time. And yet, these images show our deep need to be connected to past and future, home and hoped for new beginnings, community and God.

Professor Gregory Cuéllar of Austin Presbyterian Seminary works with children who have traveled across the desert to get to the United States. He and his wife started a project called *Arte de Lágrimas* (Art of Tears). Migrant children are invited to draw their home or their journey. Cuéllar, who writes and teaches about migration and immigration as part of his study of the Old Testament, noted the powerful religious imagery in the children's art:

"The Bible and lived reality may be separated by historical distance, but in terms of the essence of those two stories, the story of the asylum-seeker today and the patriarchs, they speak to each other."*

Shoes, a staff, a meal eaten quickly; God instructs the Israelites to take the bare necessities for making the long, dangerous journey of migration to the promised land. No doubt they, too, looked around and tucked in their back-pack or pockets symbols of home, reminders of God's presence, and relentless hope in God's promised future.

Questions for Reflection

1. Have you ever had to leave your home quickly? If so, what did you take? If not, if you were forced to flee your home, what would you take with you?
2. When you hear about people leaving their homes and crossing borders, what is your reaction and why?

Prayer for the Day

God, you called your people out of oppression and slavery to make the long, arduous journey to the promised land of freedom and safety. We lament the need for so many of your children to flee their homes due to violence, war, and poverty. Grant them safety, give them respite, make for them places of welcome, bring us all to your promised place where everyone has enough and hurt and destruction are no more. Amen.

---

*Leslie Scanlon, "Children Share Asylum Journey through Art," *The Presbyterian Outlook*, December 14, 2018, https://pres-outlook.org/2018/12/children-share-asylum-journey-through-art/.

Saturday

Ephesians 6:10–17

*Stand therefore, and fasten the belt of truth around your
waist, and put on the breastplate of righteousness. As
shoes for your feet put on whatever will make you ready to
proclaim the gospel of peace.*

Ephesians 6:14–15

Shoes of Proclamation

The last time I woke up, did my morning devotion, said
my prayers, and then said to myself, "OK, let me get
dressed with the whole armor of God so as to be ready for
combat against the cosmic powers of this present darkness," was, well, never. My to-do list often wiggles its way
into my prayers for friends, family, self, and world. The
ever-present clock surfaces to my consciousness as I try
and quiet my mind, focus on God, center myself on priorities that matter. Frequently, I lift up to the Lord places
heaving with war, people reeling from inflicted violence,
oppression, and persecution. I pray, fervently at times,
but I do not envision myself enlisted in the army against

the evil, cosmic powers of this present darkness. Perhaps I should, not in the "Onward Christian Soldiers" way, but in this Ephesians style, as one dressed to proclaim the gospel of peace.

Like any good metaphor, the one described in these verses juxtaposes two images that grab our attention in their oddity. Who puts on armor in order to proclaim peace? Troops get called up to "keep the peace," but with tanks and guns at their disposal they enforce a stoppage in fighting, not usher in a peaceable kingdom where the lion and lamb snuggle and hurt and destruction are no more. This armor of God, however, enables children of the Christ child to do the arduous, ongoing, daily, endless work of peacemaking, real reconciliation, and beloved community building.

These shoes are made for preaching, and not just with words, either. We need to be dressed for discipleship from head to toe. The belt of truth. The breastplate of righteousness. Whatever footwear that works for freely spreading the Good News of Jesus Christ. The shield of faith. The helmet of salvation. And do not forget the sword of the Spirit, which is the word of God. The irony, of course, is that this holy uniform does not protect us from physical harm; instead those shoes of proclamation take us to places where we are made utterly vulnerable, putting us side by side with refugees, prisoners, the poor and oppressed. In other words, those shoes walk us smack dab in the middle of those being crushed by the cosmic powers of this present darkness in order to bear the light of Christ to the ones in deepest need of his love.

My to-do list, the relentless self-inflicted pressure of mistaking petty priorities for important ones, sputtered prayers for the world—in all of it, the Spirit, the word of God, the truth and righteousness of Jesus Christ intrudes, interrupts, prods. Submitting to that voice, rather than my own or that of the devil, marks the first step in finding the right proclamation shoes to wear each day.

Questions for Reflection

1. What difference would it make if you imagined your-self in this whole armor described in Ephesians?
2. What shoes do you need to put on in order to proclaim the gospel of peace?
3. How can you spread the gospel of peace in your spheres of influence today?

Prayer for the Day

Prince of peace, as your followers we know our call is to not only proclaim the gospel of peace, but also to embody it in every interaction and word. You have given us all we need to be mak-ers of peace and bearers of your light. As we don the whole armor of God, may others see us and be not only comforted but also inspired to join your grace-filled revolution of reconcilia-tion. Amen.

Week Six

Oil

Fifth Sunday of Lent

Psalm 23

You prepare a table before me
  in the presence of my enemies;
you anoint my head with oil;
  my cup overflows.
                            Psalm 23:5

Anointed with Oil

Bright green, lush foliage, a forest scene in spring dons the cover of a coffee-table book tucked away on one of my many bookshelves. Each page shows similar scenes. Verdant. Pastoral. Calming. Along the bottom of the photographs the words of the Twenty-third Psalm unfold in the King James Version. "The LORD is my shepherd; I shall not want" (v. 1). Maketh. Leadeth. Yea. Thou. Anointest. The antiquated language rings in my head. I anticipate the words coming on the next page. I can recite each verse from memory. I cannot count the number of times I have read this psalm with a congregation gathered for a funeral, a family huddled around a loved one's grave, a parishioner about to be wheeled into surgery or on the cusp of heaven.

The book, though, the coffee-table book that sits on a shelf, flanked by scholarly commentaries on the Bible, reminds me of one funeral—my grandfather's. He gave me the book the summer I started seminary. He wrote me a note in the front pages, indicating his prayers and his pride, his distinct angular script evidence of his attention to detail and his exacting nature. The book with its inscription felt like a familial anointing of my unexpected call to ministry. No one foresaw this path for me and many in my family, including myself, questioned its source and trajectory. But my grandfather, living too far away to give me this anointing in person, sent it through the mail.

"Yea" though I am confused and scared, unsure and unsteady and feeling unworthy, thou sendest messages by the United States Postal Service, affirming your anointing with a note, a book, a flash of lush forest, a visitation of familiar script and Scripture.

God's unmistakable care and attention, the confirmation that God hears and notices, sees us slogging through dark valleys and manifests itself in tables laden with casseroles delivered, a text saying simply, "I am praying for you this morning," or the words of someone we respect anointing us by saying, "Do not doubt God has called you."

Rarely in our modern context do we actually anoint people with oil, set them apart for a particular role by marking them on the head with a slick substance. However, sometimes we do, in confirmation or baptism, remind those being anointed and all of us witnessing it, that we belong to God, that we are God's anointed ones, called, chosen to serve, never abandoned, seen, protected, and loved. Surely goodness and mercy shall follow us all the days of our lives, and we will dwell in the house of the Lord forever.

Questions for Reflection

1. Have you ever been anointed with oil? When and why? Have you ever witnessed someone being anointed with oil? What was the context and occasion?
2. When has someone confirmed your sense of call to a particular work or service?
3. Can you remember a time when God ministered to you when you were "walking through the valley of the shadow of death"?

Prayer for the Day

Yea though I do not know what this day, or any day, will bring, I know, Lord, that thou art with me and will never leave me alone. You see me when I get up and when I lie down. There is nowhere I can go where you are not, not even the valley of the shadow of death. Help me to abide in the goodness and mercy you relentlessly provide. Help me to remember that you anointest my head with oil and therefore there is nothing I lack, nothing more I want. Amen.

Monday

Matthew 25:1–13

"Ten bridesmaids took their lamps and went to meet the bridegroom. Five of them were foolish, and five were wise. When the foolish took their lamps, they took no oil with them; but the wise took flasks of oil with their lamps."
Matthew 25:2–4

Out of Oil

What cannot be shared, borrowed, or even bought? In a culture so marked by consumerism we hardly notice the constant sales pitches bombarding us, we struggle to imagine a commodity that cannot be exchanged or purchased. This story of wise and foolish maidens, awaiting the bridegroom, antiquated as it feels, begs a very relevant question: what does God require of us that we must seek, keep, and maintain, not from others or from Amazon, but from the Spirit? What does the oil of this parable represent? Faith? The light of Christ? Morality? As the hymn puts it, we must keep our lamps trimmed and burning, but what in the world does that actually mean?

The difference between the two groups, the wise versus the foolish, entails readiness, preparedness, anticipation of required supplies for when the bridegroom arrives, regardless of how long he is delayed. Right focus equals holy wisdom. Readiness to meet Christ begins with filtering out the many distractions that beckon us to look elsewhere for purpose, affirmation, security, and abundant life. All the bridesmaids went out to meet the bridegroom. All of them got drowsy when he was nowhere to be found, all of them slept. At this point, all ten are equally righteous and finite. The tipping point comes with the bridegroom's arrival. Only the wise half thought to bring extra oil.

This seems to be the only instance in the Bible where keeping extra of something is lauded. Other passages say if you have two coats give one away; give away your shirt, too, if it is demanded of you. Don't build barns to store up your grain, your life may be demanded of you this very night. But here the instruction requires holding something back, in reserve, just in case. But what?

The answer reveals itself when we keep our focus on the bridegroom, on the coming of Jesus and the return of Christ. The question is not so much what the oil represents, but, rather, what do we need to be ready to meet Jesus at any given moment? The oil of this parable may be different for me than it is for you. The oil you need this Lent may be different next Lent. Start by focusing on the bridegroom's promised arrival—not the timing, but the fact of his certain return.

Right focus equals holy wisdom. Looking to Jesus reveals what preparedness requires. Remembering who we serve shows us the substance of the oil needed to make our light shine brightest. The oil, whatever it may be for you right now, cannot be bought, sold, bartered, or exchanged, because it is precious and priceless. The oil, even if you wished to do so, cannot be shared, but it can and will make an impact. The light of one lamp cannot be given to those lacking oil, but nevertheless it illumines the entire room.

Questions for Reflection

1. What are you running low on right now, in your life of faith? How can you replenish it?
2. Do you relate more to the wise or foolish brides-maids? When have you felt more like the wise brides-maids? Why?
3. Do you often think about Jesus' promised return? If you knew you would meet Jesus today, how would you prepare?

Prayer for the Day

Lord, distractions of every kind overwhelm us. Busyness. Stress. Fear. Worry. Comparing ourselves to others. When we try and quiet our minds, so much floods our consciousness that focusing on you and your will and your ways feels impossible. Send your Spirit, the Comforter, to quell the noise within and without so that we might know what oil we need to keep our lamps burning brightly with the light of Jesus Christ. Amen.

Tuesday

Matthew 26:6–13

Now while Jesus was at Bethany in the house of Simon the leper, a woman came to him with an alabaster jar of very costly ointment, and she poured it on his head as he sat at the table.

Matthew 26:6–7

Expensive Oil

Sanctuary renovations. Capital campaigns. Annual budgets, both church and personal. Allocation of endowment funds. The debate about contingency funds, to have one or not to have one, if there is one, what balance represents a faithful amount to be held in reserve? Questions about money bring to the surface deeply held opinions and deeply felt emotions. In one church I served, an outspoken leader would argue mightily for a bottom-line budget of zero—money in, money out. A church, he said, should never hold back funds but should use what was needed for expenses and give away the rest to missions. Another equally vocal member of the church board felt passionately that reserve funds meant prudence—the ability to "fix the aging furnace" should it fail. (Is every church's furnace on the brink of collapse?) The rest of the governing body guided us to a middle ground, if not a happy medium.

Then, of course, there are the great debates around pipe organs: their crucial nature for worship versus the utter wastefulness of spending a million dollars renovating them. Same for stained glass windows or expensive art on the church parlor walls or bringing the decor of the fellowship hall into the twenty-first century, or at least the twentieth century. What about an elevator? Extravagance or a necessity for welcoming those with mobility challenges? And then there are the mission trips to far-away places. Does the cost justify the service or are we better off sending a check?

This story from Matthew could be set in any church, in any place, in any tradition. What is wasteful extravagance and what is a faithful use of the resources we have, from oil to endowments? This story from Matthew could be set around any kitchen table, with any family attempting to be good stewards of whatever resources they have at their disposal. I remember vividly a conversation with a fellow Presbyterian attending a workshop on stewardship telling me how angry his father would get at his mother for taking a portion of their family's crops and chicken's eggs to the pastor. What his mother saw as faithful, his father saw as foolish.

Jesus, ever mindful of the poor, of the vulnerable, of the hungry, praises the woman for pouring out this expensive oil, anointing him, he tells the disciples, for his looming death. Jesus recognizes that this woman recognized his status and circumstance. She knew to relinquish her most precious possession and lavish it on Jesus before the opportunity to express her love for him had passed. The heart of this story is as simple and as complicated as that. How do we unashamedly, publicly, copiously show our love to Jesus? How do we offer our best to him out of gratitude and joy? How do we hold nothing in reserve for the sake of our Savior?

Perhaps such displays involve expensive oil, or a pipe organ, or writing checks, or telling our faith story in worship, or reconciling with the person we least want to forgive. Whatever we offer freely, pour out completely, and give to Jesus in love, others will notice and Jesus will remember.

Questions for Reflection

1. Have you ever participated in discussions about what is faithful to spend and on what? How did you discern the answer to those questions?
2. When have you anointed Jesus with expensive oil, lavishly giving your very best out of love for him?
3. What are you holding back from Jesus?

Prayer for the Day

Jesus, you remember. You remember us. You honor what we offer in love, be it expensive oil or a heartfelt lament. When we come to you unashamed and pour ourselves out in love or fear or doubt or praise, you welcome us. You know us. You remember us. When we feel as if we have nothing to give, you embrace us and tell us we are enough. You remember us, even when we forget you. Thanks be to God. Amen.

Wednesday

Luke 10:25–37

"But a Samaritan while traveling came near him; and when he saw him, he was moved with pity. He went to him and bandaged his wounds, having poured oil and wine on them."

Luke 10:33–34a

Oil of Compassion

No matter how many times I read or hear this story, the physicality of the Samaritan's compassion touches me. The priest and the Levite go to the other side of the road, they literally distance themselves from the wounded man in the ditch. The Samaritan goes closer, moved by pity. He gets down into the ditch with the suffering traveler. The text says, "He went to him and bandaged his wounds, having poured oil and wine on them" (v. 34). The hands-on care continues as the Samaritan transports the man to the inn and cares for him there. He provides funds for ongoing care and promises to return. All for a stranger. No wonder the lawyer answers Jesus with such speed and clarity when asked, "Which of these three, do you think, was a neighbor to the man who fell into the hands of the robbers?" Obvious to even the lawyer who wanted to justify himself, the unequivocal answer is: "The one who showed him mercy" (v. 36–37a).

Just as the cruelty of the robbery entailed physical, close contact, so does the mercy that seeks to amend the injuries and pain. Healing cannot happen from a distance. Compassion moves us to act, to get into the ditch, to pour oil on wounds and bandage them, to ensure the person brutalized and violated knows another side to humanity, to strangers.

In the summer of 2017, while living in Charlottesville, Virginia, I participated with other faith leaders in offering a counter witness to what was deemed "the summer of hate"—when neo-Nazis and white supremacists rallied in the streets of our university town. The events of August 12 of that year turned Charlottesville from a place into an event. White supremacists, neo-Nazis, and a myriad of counterprotesters converged, and chaos and violence ensued. The experience marked a turning point in my own life of faith, facing the undeniable reality of deadly hate directed at Jews, African Americans, and anyone deemed not white by those chanting "blood and soil." Those events removed the naive scales from my eyes. Scales too many of my neighbors never had the luxury of wearing. Physical brutality invaded the streets. People were beaten, pepper sprayed, pelted with bottles of urine. My neighbors were terrorized. The physical beauty of compassion, though, refused to relent, even in the midst of AK-47s, cruel chants, and real and present danger. Strangers intervened, putting their bodies between those threatened with fists and weapons. Strangers set up tents and cradled in their laps those whose eyes burned with pepper spray, pouring water over their faces, wiping them dry with towels and their own shirts. Strangers huddled in prayer with those afraid, weeping, distraught. Those moved with pity went into the ditch, toward the suffering, and showed mercy. On that weekend of hate, countless people also became neighbors. The oil of compassion flowed in those violent streets. Frankly, we need more of it in *all* our streets.

Questions for Reflection

1. When have you been moved with pity to go toward someone in the ditch, literally or figuratively? What did you do once you got there?
2. Have you ever been physically cared for by a stranger? When has someone poured oil and wine on your wounds?
3. Who has been a neighbor to you? To whom are you a neighbor?

Prayer for the Day

Jesus, this very day, you are calling us to be neighbors to someone in need of mercy. As we go about our tasks and routines, help us to see those suffering in the ditch. Strengthen our faith in you in order to embolden us to move toward our neighbors in need of compassion. If we find ourselves wounded and afraid, send Samaritans to minister to us. May each encounter of this day make manifest our love for you and for our neighbors. Amen.

Thursday

James 5:13–18

Are any among you suffering? They should pray. Are any cheerful? They should sing songs of praise. Are any among you sick? They should call for the elders of the church and have them pray over them, anointing them with oil in the name of the Lord.

James 5:13–14

Healing Oil

The power of prayer. Christians talk a lot about the power of prayer, the importance of prayer, the practice of prayer. We say frequently, "You are in my prayers," or "I am holding you in prayer." Like much of the culture, we too repeat the oft-used and often empty phrase, "thoughts and prayers." We may discuss our prayer life with close confidants. We may confess our struggle to focus when we attempt to pray. But how often do we share the times when prayer truly transformed? Do we really believe what James says in these verses, that the prayer of the righteous is powerful and effective? How often do communities of faith gather for the express purpose of praying for a person or a situation?

Jesus instructs us to ask in order to receive, tells his disciples that faith the size of a mustard seed moves mountains. Too often I forget his teaching and promise. Too often I fall into hopelessness and neglect the gift and power of prayer. I need the righteous, the mature in faith, the elders, deacons, and pastors to pray with and for me, especially when I do not know what to pray or cannot bring myself to pray. Those prayers are indeed healing and effective, no matter if the physical sickness persists, the perplexing situation remains, and questions of what comes next go unanswered.

Early in my ministry, a beloved couple in the church and community got devastating news. Their child had leukemia. The entire congregation felt the weight of their pain. Friends rallied. Food appeared at their door. Many people asked: What can we do? How can we help? Pray. Please pray. Yes, yes, of course. We will pray. We are praying. And we did pray. Individually, in worship, in Sunday school classes. The news came that the date had been set for a bone marrow transplant, thanks be to God, a match found. Please pray. Someone in the congregation, I cannot remember who, came to the leaders of the church and said we need to pray, together, while the transplant took place. A group planned a vigil for the sanctuary, sending out a schedule for people to sign up so that at every moment of that hopeful and harrowing day, prayers of the faithful would be ascending to the throne of grace. All the time slots filled quickly. Our prayers flowed like oil, spoken, silent, written, spontaneous, nonstop for hours.

Word came that the transplant went well. Prayers kept going. Meals kept coming. The oil of hope, if not gladness, anointed this family. As I write this, the cancer remains gone. The child of this church, well. Thanks to modern medicine and, yes, prayer. Had the outcome been tragically different, however, I would insist that the prayers were effective and healing, because not only did that family feel the love of God through the prayers of the righteous, all of us also experienced the transformative power of the Holy Spirit as we poured out our hopes together.

Questions for Reflection

1. Have you ever gathered with a group of believers to pray for a specific person or situation? What was that experience like for you?
2. Is it meaningful or empty to tell someone you are praying for them or to have someone tell you that you are in their thoughts and prayers?
3. Do you believe that the prayer of the righteous is powerful and effective?

Prayer for the Day

Lord Christ, you teach us to pray, tell us to ask and we will receive. And yet often we think our concerns too trivial to warrant your attention, or we doubt our ability to ask rightly, or we even question your will to intervene. Help us for just a few moments today to embrace the gift of prayer, of talking honestly with you, of pouring out our hearts in praise and pain. In your mercy, hear our prayers. Amen.

Friday

Numbers 4:16

Eleazar son of Aaron the priest shall have charge of the oil for the light, the fragrant incense, the regular grain offering, and the anointing oil, the oversight of all the tabernacle and all that is in it, in the sanctuary and in its utensils.

Numbers 4:16

Oil for Worship

"The oil stung my eyes. I kept blinking, trying to see." My teenage daughter, newly confirmed, now a full member of the church, described the experience as mildly, unexpectantly, irritating. The tradition at the congregation of her confirmation included each confirmand kneeling, a blessing written specifically for that budding adult spoken as the sign of the cross was made on their foreheads. Apparently, the pastor anointing my middle child used a generous portion of oil, so much, in fact, that it dripped down her face and into her eyes. My child, one of gentle and shy temperament, sought not to call any more attention to herself than the kneeling, blessing, and anointing already had, so she refused to wipe off the oil and allowed it to run where gravity and the curve of her face took it.

At first, I lamented that the most noteworthy aspect of this meant-to-be-special worship service was this complaint about the oil. The oil, so rarely used in our tradition, was to be particularly meaningful, memorable, a mark of their new status, their new phase of faith. The blessing, carefully crafted for each eighth grader, I had hoped would stick with her, guide her days, help her to live into the promises she'd publicly made that morning. Hence, I asked with anticipation how she experienced the service and got, "The oil stung my eyes. I kept blinking, trying to see."

Oil for worship keeps the light burning in the temple. Oil for worship anoints the people for service. Oil for worship marks a change in role or status. Oil for worship makes the light of God visible to worshipers and outsiders alike. Oil for worship, precious and vital, gets assigned a keeper, one with a name—Eleazar, son of Aaron the priest—so that accountability can be tracked, bottles replenished, reserves kept. Oil for worship should be meaningful, memorable, noteworthy for all it represents to God and to the people. Oil for worship marks a change that is significant, causes some discomfort, disorients us, maybe mars our vision, and gives us new eyes with which to see.

"He was generous with the oil," my maturing daughter added. Oil for worship ought to be used generously, too. Like the psalms say about goodness and mercy and cups overflowing, the precious oil poured on the head overflows and runs down Aaron's beard, down the collar of his robe. The oil for light and anointing ought to be so obvious and impactful that it elicits blinking until we have eyes to see.

My teenager will never forget the worship service in which she declared her faith in Jesus Christ and promised to participate in his church. The kneeling, the blessing, and the oil all set her apart for service. Even today, years later, if I ask her about that morning, the thing she remembers most is the oil—the liberal amount of oil used in worship that ran down her face, into her eyes, and stung, changing her vision in ways she is still discovering.

Questions for Reflection

1. Have you ever been anointed with oil? If so, what were the circumstances? How did it feel? If not, can you imagine occasions when it would be meaningful to be anointed or to anoint another with oil?
2. What items are crucial for worship? If not oil, what? Water? Bread? Wine? A piano, organ, Bible? Who takes care of these things? What would happen if they were not there one Sunday?
3. When does your congregation use light in worship? Candles in the chancel? Christmas Eve? What does this light symbolize to you?

Prayer for the Day

Lord God, you send the light of the world, Jesus Christ, that no darkness can overcome. You call us to let our light shine. You tell us to not hide our light under the bushel basket. Despite our finitude and failings you set us apart for service, calling us to be the light of the world, too. When the oil of our anointing stings and we feel disoriented, unsure what to do or where to go, assure us of your Holy Spirit, present, working through us, comforting us until you yourself wipe every tear from our eyes. Amen.

Saturday

Exodus 29:1–9

You shall take the anointing oil, and pour it on [Aaron's]
head and anoint him.

Exodus 29:7

Oil for Consecration

The word *consecration* rarely comes up in casual conversation. Even in church settings talk of consecrating someone
or something garners attention due to its infrequency. In
my tradition we ordain minister and elders. The worship
service of ordination includes the asking of questions and
the laying on of hands. No oil. Ordination is described as
commissioning or dedicating, not generally as consecration. Nonetheless, the ceremony, at least in my branch of
the vine, requires preparation, the making of promises,
prayer, kneeling, and the surprisingly weighty experience
of having others put their hands on your head, shoulders,
back, and arms while prayers for the Spirit are evoked.
Often Communion is celebrated, the bread and wine set
apart, consecrated for sacred use.

Set apart for sacred service. At base, the definition of consecration seems straightforward. Oil, bread, bulls, priests, all set apart for sacred purposes, to be used in worship and useful to our God. The clothing, whether robe and stole, alb and rope belt, miter and staff, collar and cross, all outward signs of divine calling, inward identity, singular purpose: to be used and useful. The public nature of both the service and the vestments, the oil and bread, the bull and blood, make for accountability and reveal the communal nature of sacred service. None of the pomp and circumstance is for its own sake or for the sake of the ones at the center of it. All of the elements and words, songs and oaths, processions and promises, are for the sake of God's good plan for the world.

But what about those who've not had oil poured over their heads or hands laid on their shoulders? What about those wearing scrubs or public works uniforms, business suits or sweats stained with baby spit-up? Are only priests given sacred purpose? No. The priesthood of all believers requires each and every one of us to be used and useful for the sake of God's good plan for the world. Our baptismal vocation sets us apart for sacred service.

We may be consecrated with the oil of spilled paint in an elementary school classroom or spilled blood in an emergency room. The oil that sets us apart for service may be ink on our fingers or the smell of chopped onions on our hands. The oil of consecration could smell of bleach from cleaning bathrooms or antiseptic from tending to the wounds of others. The clothing that reveals our calling comes in countless forms, from clerical robes to denim overalls. God calls us all to serve, setting us apart to be the light of the world and the salt of the earth.

Questions for Reflection

1. Have you participated in a service of ordination or consecration? If so, what was the experience like for you? What do you remember about it?
2. What does the oil of consecration look like for your calling? What "vestments" do you wear as you serve God?

Prayer for the Day

God, you call each of us to serve you. You give us gifts to share. You work through our particular temperaments and skills, so much so that we sometimes fail to see that our work and passions, our inclinations and curiosities, all fulfill your purposes for us and for your beloved world. We ask only to be useful, to and for you. Amen.

Holy Week

Coats, Towels, and Thorns

Palm Sunday

Luke 19:29–40

As [Jesus] rode along, people kept spreading their cloaks on the road.

Luke 19:36

Coats on the Road

The disciples sent to fetch the colt for Jesus' entry into Jerusalem are the first in this passage to relinquish their cloaks. They remove their coats and cast them over the colt so that Jesus does not ride bareback into town. The crowds follow suit and spread their cloaks on the road, creating a path worthy of the one riding upon it. More than a red carpet, more than clearing the streets for a president or visiting dignitary, the crowd gives up their own coats to show their reverence for Jesus of Nazareth. The cheering crowds offer up their cloaks willingly to the one who instructs his followers to give the shirts off their back to those who would take their coats. As if practicing what will be required of those who follow fully, disciples and crowds alike give whatever they have to show their love and loyalty to Jesus. Their enthusiasm and joy at Jesus' arrival overcomes any impulse to hold back emotions or resources.

On this Palm Sunday, how do we respond like those who spread their coats on the road before Jesus? Too often we suppress both our praise and our generosity. We fear looking foolish. We calculate the cost of our giving. We value the protection of our coats over the worship of our Lord. We justify standing in the back, observing the parade, wrapped tightly in our cloak by saying things like "there are enough coats on the road already" or "if Jesus really needs it, I will give it to him." Jesus himself tells the Pharisees that if the crowds did not shout, the stones would. When we hold back our cries of "hosanna" and cling to our coats, creation sings, and the streets overflow with palms and songs. Jesus still enters triumphantly into Jerusalem, with or without our coat on the road ahead of him.

The loss when we reserve our garment and squelch our shouts is mostly ours. I know a person who died suddenly, his dresser drawers filled with unworn clothing, boxes of brand-new shoes lining his closet floor. Many of the pristine shirts and sweaters had been gifts from friends and family. He justified holding them in reserve because he wanted to save them for a special occasion. He died before that occasion materialized, never enjoying the gift, never giving those who gave them the pleasure of seeing him wear them. But in the months before his sudden death he started to share his feelings more openly. For much of his life he had held his emotions under tight control, handing out affirmation and expressions of affection sparingly. Something in him moved him to tell those closest to him that he loved them. His unmitigated, unmeasured words of affirmation and care meant the world to those he left behind.

Palm Sunday is no time to hold back. Shout with abandon. Praise Jesus with song and prayer. Throw your coat into the mix, spread it on the road. Do not suppress your urge to be generous with your affection, your resources, your love. Jesus will not walk the earth forever. The time is now.

Questions for Reflection

1. What are you holding back from Jesus? From others? Why are you holding it in reserve?
2. Where else in Luke's Gospel do you find the word "cloak" or "coat"? How do these passages inform your understanding of this Palm Sunday reading?
3. When have you been moved to throw your coat on the road? In other words, when have you given away something with abandon, without calculating the cost or worrying about the consequences? What happened?

Prayer for the Day

Lord Jesus, today of all days, I shout with joy that you have come into the world and come into my life. Your compassion for me and for all creation stuns me. What can I give to show my gratitude? My desire to follow you? My love for you? You do not desire sacrifices, but ask instead for a contrite heart and unrestrained worship. In thanksgiving and praise, I spread my coat on the road before you, a symbol of my hope to hold nothing back from you who gave everything for me. Amen.

Monday

Exodus 28:1–5

These are the vestments that they shall make: a breastpiece, an ephod, a robe, a checkered tunic, a turban, and a sash. When they make these sacred vestments for your brother Aaron and his sons to serve me as priests, they shall use gold, blue, purple, and crimson yarns, and fine linen.

Exodus 28:4–5

Ritual Coats

My grandmother sewed many of my clothes when I was a child. I attended a Catholic elementary school, my sister and I among the few Protestants students in the mix. Uniforms entailed a lot of wool in dark colors. We lived in Halifax, Nova Scotia, and even now, years and years later, the smell of wet wool transports me to the fluorescent lit halls of the school located a few blocks and across the street from our apartment. I hated the itch of the tights, the boring navy so dark it looked black on our skirts, the strictly practical leather lace-up shoes. No matter, the dress code rules could not be bent. Resistance was futile. But mass days provided fashion respite, a break from the ordinary, a chance to don what I deemed beautiful: a white dress. Not just any white dress either, a white dress sewn especially for me by my grandmother.

It being the early seventies, the fabric consisted of a double-knit polyester, but at least it was not wool. The sheen a bonus from my perspective, the cut a simple A-line. And the pièce de resistance? A grosgrain ribbon adorned with tiny pink and blue flowers running from the neck to the hem. I loved this dress. It marked a special occasion with every celebration of Mass. No matter that neither my sister nor I could receive Communion. We could, though, dip our fingers in the holy water at the entrance to the sanctuary. We could marvel at the ornate altar and the stained glass windows. We could temporarily escape the humiliation of spelling bees and multiplication drills. We could wear a garment of beauty made with love taken out of the closet and worn only on high and holy days.

The clothing, while a dress and not a checkered coat, marked both the time and the purpose, the place and the person. When all of us lined up to walk through the convent that was otherwise off-limits to us, we looked different than on other days, an array of white dresses, similar but distinct, anticipating the candles and incense, the mystery and the reverence. I feel the same way when I put on my black Geneva gown on Sunday mornings and thread the liturgically appropriate colored stole through the small rope on the back. I am myself, but different. Prepared for a role that uses my gifts and skills but also transcends them in ways I do not understand. I wonder if medical professionals feel that way about their scrubs or business people their suits or scientists their lab coats or firefighters their helmets.

Our outer garments, coats, jackets, clerical collars, name tags, badges—all immediately signal to the world our role and purpose. What, then, are our ritual coats, those outer characteristics that demonstrate to the world that we are followers of Jesus? How will people know when they see us that Jesus is our Lord and teacher? Perhaps we could choose a small symbol of our faith to wear daily to remind us to make our allegiance to the triune God obvious, not just on high holy occasions, but always.

Questions for Reflection

1. Do you or have you ever worn clothing that reflected your role or job? If so, did people respond to you differently when you wore it? How did you feel about being identified by those garments?
2. What outward items reveal your current responsibilities? How are they connected to what you do?
3. Do you wear special clothing to worship? Why or why not?

Prayer for the Day

We are those who are first and foremost clothed in Christ. No matter our other uniforms, the simplicity or ornateness of our other garments, nothing is more beautiful than being wrapped in the love of our Lord and showing that love to others. Help us, we pray, to make our discipleship undeniably visible to the world in everything we say and do. Amen.

Tuesday

Genesis 37:1–11

Now Israel loved Joseph more than any other of his children, because he was the son of his old age; and he had made him a long robe with sleeves.

Genesis 37:3

Coats of Favor

Family stories shape us, often unknowingly. Our work ethic or inability to tolerate rudeness, our need for success or our views of money, how we interact with strangers and family members alike, all this can be passed down from generation to generation. The stories of our family, known or not, are often the conduit for that inheritance. The writer of Genesis tells us: *"This is the story of the family of Jacob"* (v. 1, emphasis added). Interestingly, the family story of Jacob begins with seventeen-year-old Joseph. The baby. The favored youngest son. The cocky adolescent foolish enough to snitch on his older brothers and then tell them his dreams of ruling over them. The teenager parading around in the ostentatious coat bestowed upon him by his doting father. This is the story of the family of Jacob and the family of Jacob, in modern terms, demonstrates obvious dysfunction.

Jacob plays favorites. Joseph's brothers hate him. Joseph's older brothers hate him because he is so clearly their father's favorite, and they hate him even more because of his words, his dream of ruling over the family—the youngest usurping the role of the patriarch. Jealousy rules. Soon brothers will plot against brother and then lie to their father about it. That coat of favor will become evidence of both the crime and the cover-up. Estrangement will be a theme of this family story, taking up many chapters. This is the story of the family of Jacob, the family God chooses, the family God will use to further salvation history. All of which is to say, we ought to feel comfort in knowing that God works through *all* our families' stories, even the most painful and dysfunctional among them.

Jacob could not know the impact of that heartfelt gift. He did not understand that the coat of many colors or the robe with long sleeves, that outer garment that would set his youngest apart, would exacerbate the gulf between his children. Joseph, that seventeen-year-old boy, did not imagine his favored status would get him thrown in a pit and carried off to Egypt. Even the older brothers who so hated the overconfident teen never foresaw the suffering they would bring to the father they loved. Family stories are like that: messy, full of inadvertent hurts, littered with seasons of estrangement, punctuated by tears of joy and sorrow.

We walk around in the coat our father gave us, oblivious to the impact our wearing it has on those closest to us. We keep our youngest's words in mind but fail to recognize that our other children need to know we understand their frustration with their brother. We live the stories told and kept secret, unaware that they move us to act in ways we will come to regret. God indeed works through all our families and all of our stories, the chapters of triumph and the ones where we hit rock bottom. God also gives us the ability to recognize the power, both good and not so good, of the coats we give and receive, wear and steal, treasure and disdain. The story of the family of Jacob ends with reconciliation. Our family story, through Jesus Christ, does too. God's salvation story has the power to shape every family narrative not only in the end, but right now.

Questions for Reflection

1. Have you ever received a special gift from a family member? What was it? How did you feel about receiving it? How did other family members respond to the gift? Have you ever given such a gift?
2. What are some of the stories of *your* family? What do they reveal about your family's values? Are they stories you want to continue to live or do you want to change them?
3. When have you experienced a family estrangement? Did reconciliation happen? If so, how? If not, why not?

Prayer for the Day

Gracious God, you work through ordinary people, choose to tell your salvation story through complicated families, refusing to give up on us even when we hurt one another deeply. As we consider our own family stories, we see both beauty and pain. We know we have loved well but also hurt those we love the most. Forgive us. Bring reconciliation. Use the seasons of joy and the seasons of confusion to bring us all closer to you and more tightly bound to each other. Amen.

Wednesday

Matthew 5:38–42

> *"If anyone strikes you on the right cheek, turn the other also; and if anyone wants to sue you and take your coat, give your cloak as well."*
>
> Matthew 5:39b–40

Give Your Coat

Generosity is undeniably laudable, sacrificial, a noble goal. But going above and beyond the already unjust demands of an oppressor cannot be what Jesus instructs in this passage. Have not texts like "turn the other cheek" been used to justify abuse and keep people in relationships they surely ought to flee? I admit, these verses from Matthew make me anxious. Knowing that the Bible gets twisted to justify horrific, systemic oppression of entire peoples, I get nervous about echoing Jesus' words to turn over your coat to the very person who took the shirt off of your back. I mull over policies that resulted in neighborhoods being destroyed in order to build freeways. I cannot help but think about those long seasons in our history when all manner of tactics were used to suppress the vote of particular groups of citizens. Surely Jesus would not tell those dispossessed and marginalized people to give more to the very entities that stole from them in the first place.

Jesus works for justice, not against it. So, what's going on here in the Sermon on the Mount? If Jesus came to bring Good News to the poor and release to the captives, where does this notion of giving not just one's shirt, but one's coat, fit into the Christian narrative and our own discipleship? The message morphs depending on where we find ourselves in the story. Are we the one bringing suit or being sued? The one doing the striking or being struck? One of the challenges of this text comes in the form of honest self-evaluation. We may well be the unaware oppressor, supporting with our dollars industries that exploit workers or inflict violence. Hence, the first step of following Jesus' teaching requires serious self-reflection and honest repentance, because Jesus' unambiguous call to his followers demands love, not abuse. Disciples of Jesus Christ work for abundant life for all, not for some at the expense of others.

What about, however, when we find ourselves on a forced march or the other end of an unfair subpoena? Do we just keep walking, accepting the consequences no matter their justness? The short answer is no. Jesus never justifies abuse. Jesus calls for love. The verses right after these make the seemingly impossible demand of us to love our enemies and pray for those who persecute us. While we work to end violence, while we champion practices and policies that contribute to the well-being of the least of these, while we confront evil and seek to do good, we must never lose sight that Jesus loves even those who nail him to a cross, and asks God to forgive them even as he suffers at their hands. Our prayers and our hopes and our goals must reflect the radical love of Jesus Christ for all people. Just as Jesus came not to condemn the world, but to save it, we strive not to condemn, but to extend grace and mercy, even to those who treat us with contempt.

Of all Jesus' commands, teachings, and instructions, the one at the heart of giving our coat, too, may perhaps be the most difficult. We desire some form of karma or retaliation, revenge or comeuppance. Jesus tells us instead to long for, and work toward, reconciliation.

Questions for Reflection

1. How do you inadvertently participate in the oppression of others? How can you take steps to stop participating in those systems that take not only others' coats, but their shirts too?
2. Have you ever experienced wanting someone to get "what they deserve"? Or wanted to retaliate for some injustice or hurtful act? What did you do and why?
3. Who do you need to work toward reconciliation with this Lent? How can you begin that work?

Prayer for the Day

Jesus, following your teaching demands more than we can muster. You know our weaknesses, our tendencies to hurt others, our deep-seated desire for retaliation or even, at times, revenge. You recognize that without you we cannot turn the other cheek, go the extra mile, or hand over our coat. Thankfully, you promise the gift of your Holy Spirit, the Comforter, who guides, gives us the words, and empowers us to act in ways that show your love, even to our enemies. Amen.

Maundy Thursday: Towels

John 13:1-15

During supper Jesus, knowing that the Father had given
all things into his hands, and that he had come from God
and was going to God, got up from the table, took off his
outer robe, and tied a towel around himself.
John 13:2b-4

Towels around Our Waists

I turned the corner, headed to the elevator with my luggage, ready to go home after yet another work trip, when I noticed the housekeeper's cart in the hall. Large, cumbersome, stacked with little soaps, shampoo bottles, coffee supplies, linens, towels—and Bibles. The juxtaposition caught my attention. There tucked between the hand towels and the bath towels was the Word of the Lord, tenfold. I dropped my bags and took a picture with my cell phone. I wanted to remember the power of that image, but at the time I did not equate the visual with Maundy Thursday. Only after reading this story from John again did I make the connection and realize that towels and the Bible ought to be side by side and portable.

That morning in the hotel I thought mostly about the people pushing those carts up and down the hallways, doing physical work for not much pay. I thought about the time I left a whopping five-dollar tip and came back to the room, now clean and tidy, to find a note that read, "Thank you. Have a blessed day, Rhonda." Two smiley faces adorned the hotel sticky pad. The note served as a tangible reminder that the people pushing those carts and cleaning others' toilets were individuals with names and stories. Many, no doubt, fellow disciples who knew intimately and daily what it feels like to pick up a towel and serve. Perhaps that is why Jesus says the last will be first.

Jesus, during this last meal with his closest friends, with hours left of his earthly life, takes a towel, gets on his knees, and washes the disciples' feet, even the disciple who soon will betray him. The Word and the towel, together, inextricable, in Jesus and, Jesus says, in us. Maundy Thursday means that followers of Jesus serve. We are servants, servants of the Lord of all, who willingly ate with sinners, touched lepers, welcomed children, and washed feet. Nothing is beneath us when Jesus is the rock upon which we stand. No one is "less than," because Jesus died for all. If we do not put the Word alongside the towel and take them both door to door, house to house, town to town, to the ends of the earth, we are failing to follow Jesus. If we forget that those who push heavy carts down long hallways or wake up before dawn to pick up trash or get on their knees to scrub floors or carefully wash the feet of the sick for very little pay, if we forget that they have names and stories, we fail to follow the One who not only knows them by name, but numbers the hairs on their heads.

On this Maundy Thursday, pick up a towel—you can find it right alongside the Word of our Lord—and get moving.

Questions for Reflection

1. When have you served someone in a physical way, fed someone, or washed someone? Who was it? Has anyone served you in a physical way? What was that like for you?
2. Have you ever participated in a foot-washing service? What was meaningful about it? Or uncomfortable? If you have not done this, find a foot-washing service to attend.
3. Today, every time you use a towel, be reminded of Jesus' instruction to wash others' feet.

Prayer for the Day

Servant Lord, on this day we remember your meal with your friends, your words of teaching, and your act of tender love. You, Lord of all, humble yourself and wash the feet of friend and betrayer alike. You hold back nothing for our sake and we are awed by your grace. We seek only to be more and more like you each day, taking up a towel and sharing your Word, so that through our love the world will know we follow you. Amen.

Good Friday: Thorns

John 19:1–11

Then Pilate took Jesus and had him flogged. And the soldiers wove a crown of thorns and put it on his head, and they dressed him in a purple robe.

John 19:1–2

Crown of Thorns

The crown of thorns placed on Jesus' head completes the wardrobe designed to mock and humiliate him. Look at the one who says he is king of the Jews. Here he stands, beaten, powerless, and foolish. Here is the man, the one in whom Pilate finds no fault, the one the frenzied crowd calls to crucify. I have read or heard this story countless times, and I wince at the image of Jesus donning the purple robe and crown of thorns every time. I picture Mary, Jesus' mother, witnessing her son's suffering, unable to intervene. I wonder what Jesus feels beneath his calm words to Pilate. The whole scene makes my stomach turn, not only because Jesus suffers, but because I know such cruelty still exists, inflicted on people all around the world. The darkest part of our humanness too often still prevails, and yet Jesus goes to the cross for us anyway. The striking truth of Good Friday lies in that reality: human beings still humiliate, mock, and crucify one another, but God loves us, Jesus dies for us, the Spirit intercedes for us anyway.

If we do not confess the painful truth of our own complicity and participation in the ugliest sin imaginable, we cannot fathom the monumental scale of God's goodness and grace. If we fail to acknowledge our role in perpetuating evil, we too mock Jesus rather than weep at his fate.

One of my children, for many years, confused "black Friday" with Good Friday. I would remind her that black Friday was the big sale day after Thanksgiving and Good Friday the day Jesus went to the cross. "Yes, yes, right," she replied. Adding, "But shouldn't the day Jesus died be called black Friday, not good Friday? What's good about Jesus being killed?" Black Friday, in her mind, was a much more apt description of the day Jesus was crucified. A valid observation, to be sure. I would reiterate to her that the "good" of Good Friday was not Jesus' death, but what God accomplished through it: the forgiveness of sin, the victory over death, the reconciliation of the world.

That crown of thorns, designed to mock, represents the suffering servant who came to save. The Friday that goes black in the middle of the day marks the time when the light of the world overcomes all darkness. The purple robe of humiliation wraps all humanity in the love of God. The good of the One on the cross restores the God-created goodness of each one of us. Today is Good Friday, when we know without doubt the radical, transformative, saving grace of God who takes on the sin of the world, for our sake, even though we cry, "Crucify him!"

Questions for Reflection

1. What does Good Friday mean to you?
2. What moves you most about this scene between Jesus, Pilate, and the crowd?
3. Take some time to look at artistic renderings of this story. What strikes you about those depictions?

Prayer for the Day

Lord, on this Good Friday, we repent of all the ways we partici-pate in perpetuating cruelty. We confess how often we dismiss our complicity with evil. We turn our heads, unable to look at suffering, when instead we are called to see fully what our sin has wrought. On this Good Friday, we recognize the depth of our sin in order to receive and rejoice in the expanse of your grace. Amen.

Holy Saturday: Thorns

Isaiah 7:23–25

On that day every place where there used to be a thousand vines, worth a thousand shekels of silver, will become briers and thorns.

Isaiah 7:23

Thorns and Briars

We stood in the narthex, my ten-year-old son and I, the sanctuary dark except for the lone light illuminating the pulpit Bible. The last reading of the Good Friday Tenebrae service was completed and a dramatic banging sound representing the nails in Jesus' hands and feet echoed through the space. A heavy silence fell. My son leaned close and asked, "Where is the hope, Mom?" I mistakenly told him prior to worship that despite the painful subject matter, the service ended with a glimmer of hope. I wanted to reassure him. I did not want this dramatic series of reading and increasing darkness to overwhelm his ten-year-old self. In the moment that his pleading question hung in the air, I knew I'd misled him. I leaned down and whispered, "It's coming."

The last reader extinguished the last light and the congregation slowly, quietly, exited into the night. Where was the hope? I had not lied to my son, not intentionally, but I should have told him the truth. Hope indeed was coming, but not on Friday and not on Saturday either. Those of us on the other side of Easter, we know death does not get the final word, that resurrection triumphs, but on Friday night and Saturday morning and all through Saturday night, hope evades our perception. Jesus says, "It is finished." Hope peers through that seemingly final word. The Greek gives a hint, implying not so much an end, but a completion. Jesus' earthly work is complete. Salvation won, resurrection on the way. But on Friday, when the last light goes dark, and on Saturday, when the stone seals the tomb and night falls yet again, hope remains hidden.

Thorns and briars pervade the landscape. Desolation rules where once lush vineyards grew. Buried beneath the painful brambles, rich soil might yet be tilled to the surface and new crops planted, but not now. In these long hours when death and schism and estrangement and cruelty appear to win, all we can do is plead for a glimpse of hope.

Where is the hope? It is coming. While we languish in grief, feel the prick of loss, the scrape of utter isolation, we seek others who will sit with us in our fear and pain. Holy Saturday, that space between hope, calls for stalwart community, companions who will accompany us in our dark night of the soul and pledge to not leave us alone. Today is a day for holding the hand of those asking in earnest, "Where is the hope?" Today is the day we say with utter honesty, "It is coming, but we can't yet see it."

Questions for Reflection

1. When have you longed for hope but been unable to find it? What did you do during that season? Who accompanied you in that dark space?
2. Where are the places overrun with thorns and briars? Is there rich soil underneath? How can you clear the land in order to cultivate something life-giving?

Prayer for the Day

Dear God, on this Holy Saturday we look for hope, but find none. We feel the suffering of those who sit in deep darkness, afraid and at a loss for what to do. We find ourselves bereft and wondering what will come next. As we hold onto one another, we whisper in faith that hope is coming, despite all evidence that death has triumphed. May we be still and know that you are God, even now, especially now. Amen.

Easter Sunday

Stones

Easter Sunday

Luke 24:1–12

But on the first day of the week, at early dawn, they came to the tomb, taking the spices that they had prepared. They found the stone rolled away from the tomb, but when they went in, they did not find the body.

Luke 24:1–3

Moving Stones

I believe transformation is possible. This belief shapes my worldview and, I hope, my attitude and actions toward people and circumstances. I hear often the phrase, "People never change." As a follower of the Risen Christ, I simply refuse to capitulate to such fatalism. The women going that third day to Jesus' tomb expected to find a stone blocking their way to the body of their beloved teacher. Instead they encountered an open entrance. Mary Magdalene, Joanna, and Mary the mother of James brought spices and oil to anoint a dead man. Instead, two angels appeared, and the body of Jesus was nowhere to be seen. Often our anticipation of death, defeat, and endings gives way to God's plan for life, resurrection, and new beginnings. I believe transformation is possible because I follow the One who was raised from the dead and now sits on the right hand of God the Father Almighty.

Transformation happens. Not always. Not easily. Sometimes in fits and starts. But life-infused change comes to those gathered around graves prepared to dutifully execute the rituals of death. Knowing this truth urges me not to be optimistic, but to be hopeful. Remembering all Jesus taught, that he goes ahead of me to Galilee and will meet me there, calls me to act faithfully even in the face of staggeringly bad odds. I am to be a fool for Christ in the eyes of a world awash with cynicism. When others see insurmountable barriers, boulders impossible to move, people of faith see the possibility of God's glory revealed in life-giving ways. That's why we go to the grave singing, "Alleluia."

All of us encounter seemingly immovable stones. We face loss or illness, disappointment or depression, oppression or exploitation, grief or separation. Circumstances unimaginable become all too real and we feel the pain of slamming into a boulder that refuses to budge. If we remember Jesus' resurrection, and all he taught and lived, angels whisper, "Jesus is risen. Transformation happens. Death does not have the last word."

All of us, I imagine, struggle with the unanswered question of "why?" I know I do. I question God's providence, wisdom, and power in certain circumstances. Yet, knowing that the stone has been moved and Jesus lives reminds me that transformation is possible and that resurrection, even when all I see is the empty tomb, is surely coming. I intend to proclaim that truth all the way to Galilee and back, to the ends of the earth, until Jesus comes again, and everyone sees and believes.

Questions for Reflection

1. When have you faced what felt like insurmountable obstacles? What happened?
2. When have you experienced transformation? What changed and how?
3. How do you maintain hope in circumstances that leave you bereft and afraid?

Prayer for the Day

Alleluia! Christ is risen! Today we celebrate the resurrection of our Lord. Morning has broken on the dawn of redemption. Reconciliation has been won. Death has been defeated. Surely nothing is impossible for God. The stone once blocking access to our Lord has been removed, forever. No longer can anything separate us from the love of the triune God. Transformation not only is possible; through Christ's resurrection, transformation is inevitable. Rejoice, give thanks and sing! Jesus Christ is risen today! Amen.